T0164644

GOD'S POTPOURRI OF LOVE

By

Evelyn B. Ryan

Illustrations by
Heidilee Peach

Order this book online at www.trafford.com
or email orders@trafford.com

Most Trafford titles are also available at major online book retailers.

Printed in the United States of America.

ISBN: 978-1-4269-4815-2 (sc)
ISBN: 978-1-4269-4816-9 (e)

Trafford rev. 11/22/2010

 www.trafford.com

North America & international
toll-free: 1 888 232 4444 (USA & Canada)
phone: 250 383 6864 ♦ fax: 812 355 4082

CONTENTS

DEDICATIONS

I dedicate all the poems in this book to the only true God, Jehovah, the Father and His Son, Christ Jesus, because they all came from Them. I also dedicate this book to my wonderful family, my husband Charles, who has loved me since I was a child of thirteen, and with whom I have spent most of my life. To our three children, Charles, Jr., Patrick Alen, and Evelyn Marie, whom I love so very much. To my beautiful mother, Edith Marie, who loves me unconditionally, and who first brought me to Christ and has always supported my writings. To my three sisters, Iva Gene, Barbara Ann, and Leasa Juanita, to whom I have always remained close no matter how far away I was, and to my young brother, Charles, a soldier of protection in dangerous times. Thank you all for being *my Family.*

PREFACE

All of my life I have felt a closeness, a deep *connection* to a Spiritual Power. I have always felt a *Presence* moving within me in a deep place known as my *soul.* I have a real need to let that Spiritual Presence I later came to realize as "Jesus" work within me, out of my inner self through my thoughts, into my hands and off the tip of my pen. These expressions emerge as poetry, real, emotional, sensual, whether rhyming or prose. The words and feelings are what God gave to me. They are my special *gifts* from God to *you*, the reader. The product is an invitation to you, to partake of the meaning of the words, to deepen your faith, to flow toward His Presence and feel His love flowing toward your heart. If these poems touch the inner core of your being and draw you closer to God, then they have fulfilled their purpose and I have fulfilled mine...to share my love of the Father, Jehovah God, and His Son, Jesus Christ.

In this book of poems you will see into the personality of God and learn that He is a very diversified Entity. He is generous, forgiving, merciful, loving, kind, tender, patient, compassionate, and has a marvelous sense of humor. i.e. - He gave His children (mankind) the ability to laugh at himself. Without that quality, Satan might lock us in a box of depression and self-destruction with every mistake we make. I am in *awe* of the power of God.

Because God is a *diversified* Spiritual Being, I can embrace diversity too. Therefore, besides spiritual poetry, I have included poems of humor, nature poems, poems for my family, sad and happy poems, and some deep, thought-provoking poems. I hope they all give you reason to pause and put yourself into them, hopefully gleaning the feeling behind them. Ultimately, these poems are not really mine. I am just the instrument that God chose to put them on paper so that you can all enjoy them and hopefully draw closer to the Creator. As Jesus prayed, so should we. "Our Father, Who art in heaven. Holy *is* Your Name!" Amen. Amen, indeed!

"In the beginning God created the heaven and the earth. And the earth was without form, and void; and darkness was upon the face of the deep.
And the spirit of God moved upon the face of the waters."
Genesis 1:1, 2 KJV

...AND THEN THERE WAS LOVE

In the beginning there was only blackness,
a void, a nothingness. Space.
Then a finger of light split the darkness
and set a burning light in place.

Creations unending kept rolling and
set in place with blue firmament above.
Two creatures like God were created.
God smiled...and then there was *love*.

GOD'S JEWEL

God poked His finger in the clouds
to let the sunshine through.
He stirred up all the winds
and away the dark clouds blew.

He covered the earth with a blanket of green
and commanded the flowers to bloom.
He placed them in a rolling meadow
where they'd have plenty of room.

He planted the forests with thousands of pines
so they'd stay green all year 'round.
He placed the songbirds in the branches
to make a beautiful sound.

He made the butterflies full of color
and the bees to buzz the day through,
He made the mornings cool and wet
so the flowers would be kissed by dew.

He pulled the hills way up high
so they'd be called 'mountain peaks'.
Then He laid a blanket of snow up there
so it'd look pristine and neat.

He caused the mountains to weep in places
and water began to flow
and fill the streams that fed the meadows
and valleys far below.

He looked below and made the animals
and they began to roam.
He placed them just where they should be
and each one found a home.

God took another look around
at His universal space
and then He chose an empty spot
and hung *earth* in its place.

God stepped back and reassessed
and with a satisfying sigh,
proclaimed His earth a ***jewel***
hooked on *nothing* in the sky.

+ + +

"He stretched out the north over the empty place and
hanged the earth upon nothing."
Job 26:7 KJV

"The earth is the Lord's, and the fulness thereof; the world,
and they that dwell therein."
Psalm 24:1 KJV

THE BOOK OF AGES

There's a lifetime worth of wisdom
in the lines upon each page
that never seem to change as we
go from age to age.

There are stories worth the telling
of love and peace and war
that never wears from telling,
though ten thousand times and more.

There are lessons to be learned
that never seem to change
though Satan's tried for eons
the morals to rearrange.

What is this **Book of Ages**
where the wisdom is like gold,
where stories are still fresh
and never will grow old?

Just look on top the bookshelf
in any house across the land
and you'll see the world's best seller
without a print or mark of hand.

It will have the world's best cover
that will never turn to rust.
It's undisturbed, misunderstood, unread
and layered in dust.

THE FIRST DAY OF LIFE

I never knew the peace and joy
that I have felt today.
I never knew the sweet content
that envelopes me when I pray.
And then I walked in His steps
into that sacred font
of Jordon's symbolic waters.
What more could I want?

Encouragement came from every side
and loving words sincere
of "Welcome, dearest Sister,"
like music to my ears.
I could not help the feeling that
welled up in my chest.
I had worked for three long years
and tried to do my best.

At last God's Holy Spirit
made my heart so light.
I had made my decision and
I knew that it was right.
My life has just begun.
Jehovah's love is true.
I chose life in Paradise
and telling others is what I shall do.

Jehovah God is Sovereign Lord
and Christ is reigning King.
And I am beginning to realize
the happiness His Kingdom will bring.
Today I walked the Way of Peace,
each step a brand new start.
But the greatest peace I ever knew
was His love born in my heart.

Evelyn B. Ryan
Baptized
February 8, 1992

WORDS FROM GOD

My head is filled with many words
that I am urged to write.
This urgency may prod me
any time, day or night.

The subject may be varied,
be it nature, joy, or love,
but more often it is spiritual
for it originates from God above.

No matter what I'm thinking,
somehow the phrases rhyme.
The meter's not always perfect,
the words not beautiful every time.

But it seems they all have meaning,
for they are based on sight and sound.
They always express a feeling
whether I'm up or I am down.

One thing that I am sure of though,
when praises are sent my way,
the words are not really my own,
I'm the instrument for what they say.

I must give the proper credit
for the praises to God are due.
It's His words that fill my mind
and my heart echoes them too.

I can't thank Him ever enough
in the lifetime that I'm here,
so I honor Him in my writing
showing proper respect and fear.

He must send the words by angels
for they flow from off my pen.
They release a strong emotion
and a love from deep within.

I feel so grateful and humble
for I know my inner worth.
I have worked so hard to know Him
from the moment of my birth.

I pray blessings will continue
and I feel He gives me the nod.
The poems I write are His blessings,
for the words all come from God.

MAGIC MOMENTS

There are many magic moments
as we go about our day,
and some of them are heightened
when we take the time to pray.
It only takes a moment
to bow our heads in prayer
for the magic really happens
when we feel Jehovah there.
There's a magic in the laughter
that starts way down inside
when you see two squirrels a-chasing,
then find a nut to hide.
They dig with tiny fingers,
intent upon their labor,
for they'll find it in the winter
and enjoy the nutty flavor.
There is magic in the sunshine
that lifts a flowers face
or brings a butterfly from
it's nighttime hiding place.
There's magic in a bluebirds song
for he's a rare delight.
There's magic in the eagles cry
as he soars in lofty flight.
But there's a special moment
that magic can't express,
when words cannot convey
the depth of happiness.

That moment of pure magic
is at a baby's birth
when we finally realize
the extent of our true worth.
For then it finally hits us
and it's then we understand
that our blessings really flow
from an unseen Mighty Hand.
It's in the mournful melody
of the gentle mourning dove
for magic really happens
when we have learned to love.

ALONE IN SPACE

We may not be the only world
Jehovah ever made.
How can we know that we are
all alone?
There may be others just like us
who far out there have stayed
and obeyed God's Laws forever
written in stone.

Then again there may be visitors
among us here today.
They may be trying to guide us
on this earth.
They may be angels from another world
trying to lead the way
so humanity can finally realize
it's worth.

How can we know if we're alone
in this dark vast expanse?
We've come to realize
our need for God.
We can't exist alone in life
without God to enhance
our world with righteousness
and an iron rod.

MY FATHER'S WATCHIN' OVER YOU

After a long cold winter's done
when the ground begins its thaw,
the earth awakenin' to spring's
the prettiest sight this old body ever saw.

When the birds begin to twitter
and build nests high in a tree,
I fergit the miseries in my old bones
'cause the birds are a-singin' jes' fer *me*.

I watch the squirrels a-runnin'
in the treetops way up high.
And I get an extry bonus
when I see the bright sunny sky.

Then I get me down to the henhouse
to tend my cluckin' chicks.
I collect the eggs, then feed 'em.
And I gather my kindlin' sticks.

I clean my house and mend my clothes
and visit a sick friend or two.
Why, there's so much to make me happy
and a passle o' hard work to do.

The garden's gonna need a-plowin'
in a week or two or three.
And if a body comes a-callin',
why, that's where they're bound to ketch me.

But for now I spend a lot of time
readin' stories by my fire,
a-holdin' talks with my *Special Friend,*
and practicin' for His choir.

Why, jes' yesterdee I told a body
of the joy this Friend o' mine gives.
He never did understand how rich I feel
and glad each day I live.

But I gave him a *special thought*
to hold onto when day is through.
I told him in the lovin'est way I knowed,
"My Father's watchin' over YOU, too!"

JEHOVAH AND ME

Come, take my hand and walk with me
upon the *Road of Life.*
I do not want to walk this road alone.
As long as You will be my Friend,
I can handle any strife,
for You've been the Source of strength
I've never known.

You've shared with me so many things
that were so hard to bear.
Because of You I held up my own end.
It's nice to know I have the strength
because I feel You there.
You're all I need; on You I can depend.

It's good to know You're by my side
to make my paths walk straight.
I know with You I'll never fall again.
But, should I falter along the way
You'll catch me before it's too late
and help me bear up beneath Life's cruel pain.

I've never had a Friend like You
and I feel so blessed and content.
To hold Your hand means all the world to me.
To see You smile and feel You near
must be how true love is meant.
It's the balm that sets an imprisoned heart free.

There will be those who misconstrue
the meaning of what I feel.
It's sad to know they're just too blind to see.
For they'll never know the joy I do
or believe it can be real.
It's a *spiritual love* between Jehovah and me.

+ + +

"...and he came to be called 'Jehovah's friend'".
James 2:23 NWT

SIMPLICITY OF LOVE

In the shadows of the night
when time seems not to be,
I am filled with endless joy
as Jesus visits here with me.

Unfathomable peace enfolds me.
Contentment fills my soul.
His forgiveness and compassion
have once more made me whole.

And while the night blankets earth
and stars shine forth above,
my heart is humbled once again
by His *simplicity of love.*

+ + +

"...and he that loveth me shall be loved of my
Father, and I will love him, and will manifest
myself to him."
John 14:21b KJV

FLEETING TIME

You never know the time of day,
the minute or the hour
when God will judge the things you do
and knock you from your tower.

You can't foresee future events,
whether good or bad.
You'll never know what you could have done
or miss what you never had.

You'll never leave a track in life
if you don't step out bold
and grab the knowledge of the TRUTH
and wisdom while it is yet told.

For a time will come when TRUTH will be sealed
and those words won't again be spoken,
and every promise your lips have uttered
will shatter and hearts then broken.

So look up now while time rolls on
and TRUTH is within your reach,
and pay heed to the Word of God
while Someone is there to teach.

The night is fast approaching
and the light may disappear,
so grasp the knowledge of eternal life
while the wisdom of TRUTH is still here.

CRYSTAL TREES

When this morning I awakened
and viewed the world outside,
a beauty I had not seen before
lay bare before my eyes.

The world was covered in pristine snow,
trees shimmering with silver gleam,
all covered in clear icy blankets
that glistened like crystalline.

The sunshine gave the trees merit
with their silvery tinsel-like glow,
as they stood as dainty statues
all covered in ice and snow.

Oh, the joy that leapt within me
when I saw the glimmering sight
surely gives praise to Jehovah's artistry
and credit to His arm of might.

"Howbeit for this cause I obtained mercy, that in me first Jesus Christ might show forth all longsuffering, for a **pattern** to them which should hereafter believe on him to life everlasting."
1 Timothy 1:16 KJV

QUILT OF LIFE

Life is a quilted pattern
that we sew from day to day.
We sew a stitch here and there
then we put the quilt away.

Sometimes someone special
comes our way now and then,
so we add them to our pattern of life
and take out our quilt again.

There's times when our stitches get crooked,
or we lose a thread or two.
It's then we need a helping hand
to tell us what we must do.

Sometimes our helper becomes a friend
who was a stranger the day before.
Sometimes the stitches we make in life
require a great deal more.

Whatever the size and pattern we make,
it's unique to whoever we are.
For no one else can sew our quilt.
Its beauty is the best, by far.

When our quilt is finished, as it surely will be,
we'll present it to God up above.
He'll open it wide to view our pattern of life
and find each stitch was sewn with our love.

+ + +

For my mother, Edith M. Zentz, who first showed me
how to sew, then later to quilt. She has made the best
quilt of life so far.

PRAY FOR ME

When I feel my thoughts go wandering
as I kneel within the pew,
I pray for Gods sweet countenance
to wash over me anew.
I do not kneel for showiness
for all the world to see.
I kneel to ask forgiveness.
Sweet Christians...pray for me.

I kneel in quiet solitude
to thank Him for my friend,
whose strong shoulder I cry on
when my spirit threatens to bend.
An even stronger shoulder is
beside me in my prayer,
giving me His lasting strength...
thank God, Jesus is there.

Many times I falter as I
hurt the ones I love.
I kneel and make repentance
to the Glorious One above.
I hope among the multitude of
lost souls, *mine*, He'll see.
I need your help, dear neighbors,
Sweet Christians...pray for me.

+ + +

"Therefore openly confess YOUR sins to one
another and pray for one another, that YOU may
get healed. A righteous man's supplication, when
it is at work, has much force."
James 5:16 NWT

THE TREE

Something inside me turns to deep sorrow
whenever I see a tree destroyed.
It leaves a space that nothing can fill.
Its death leaves a scar, an empty void.

For years that tree struggled to grow,
roots digging deeply beneath the earth.
Its leaves cleansed the air of many pollutants.
Its branches saw many new springs birth.

A tree provides shade when summer sun scorches.
Its leaves produce oxygen cooling the air.
The foliage protects hundreds of small life beneath it,
that says with strength and protectiveness, "I care".

A tree provides warmth from its dead fallen branches
when the cold winter bites and the wind drives the snow.
It signifies strength against darkening skies,
if left where God plants it to stand tall and grow.

When winters cold fingers loosen its grip,
the buds of the leaves are a joy to see.
Nothing provides assurance that spring's on the way
than the confidence insured by the stature of a tree.

+ + +

"And the tree of the field must give its fruitage, and the land
itself will give its yield,..."
Ezekiel 34:27a NWT

THE PAINTER

He took out His paintbrush and dusted it off,
then dipped it in colors so bright,
and painted a scene breathtaking and bold
that shone even in the dark night.

There were shades of red and green and gold
that were shadowed with tan and brown.
He painted a sunset that dazzled the eyes
before He put the paintbrush down.

He opened a box of silvery dust
and sprinkled with generous hand,
a layer of frost upon the scene
of beauty across the land.

Then blowing a breath, gentle and sweet,
He created a fragrant air
that rustled the changing golden leaves
and brought Indian Summer there.

With His finger tip He touched the sun,
then flicked its gold essence away,
changing the darkness of the scene
and turning it into the day.

At last He held His painting afar
and viewed it with appraising eye.
He'd just created a golden fall,
then He bid the summer "goodbye".

WATCHERS IN THE NIGHT

They're here, though we cannot see them.
They're always near at hand.
And every soul on earth has them,
whether here or in any land.

They hear our tiniest whisper
and see each thing we may do.
God sent them to us as guardians,
to protect and comfort us, too.

They're with us every moment,
though we may not know they are there.
And Jehovah God entrusts them
with His creations every care.

They report to God of our progress.
They're part of His all-seeing eyes.
God uses them to help us
gain knowledge and learn to be wise.

And when the world would blind us,
they help us to see the Light.
They're our friends, our guardian angels.
They're the *Watchers in the night.*

+ + +

"For he shall give his angels charge over thee,
to keep thee in all thy ways."
Psalms 91:11 KJV

THE THIEF

While I lay a-sleeping,
sometime in the night,
someone stole her smile
that used to be so bright.
When I wasn't looking,
a prankster tried and true,
stole my Mothers eyes
that used to be so blue.
I took each day for granted,
not thankful for each minute
that I would have her near me,
and that she'd be with me in it.
Then I saw my own reflection.
What a shock to see a face
with lines around the eyes
that creams could not erase.
Where was this Thief of Beauty
that steals time from our life,
that changes without warning,
that adds lines of pain and strife?
Oh, if only I could gather
all the things Time took away,
the sky-blue of her eyes,
the flawless youth of yesterday.

I'd return to her the vigor
that she had so long ago.
I'd give her peace of mind
and watch her spirit grow.
I'd give her all the things
that wealth can never buy.
I'd change to pearls the teardrops
that slipped from each blue eye.
I'd return to her the wisdom
that she first gave to me.
And I'd polish it so brightly
so its truth she'd surely see.
And then the Thief of Ages
could no longer steal away
the beauty that's my Mother
for it's in my heart to stay.

LOVE IS...

Love is a gift of infinite value...
one that can neither be bought or sold.
Love can be soft, or love can be hard,
but never pretentious nor hurtful and bold.

Love should be thoughtful, caring and kind,
aware that the feelings are fragile at best.
Love isn't selfish, but always worth giving
and true love grows stronger under each test.

Love cannot be stolen or hoarded away
to savor when lonely on a cold, rainy day.
Love is a treasure that grows richer with time.
It's what songs are sung for and what makes poems rhyme.

It gives life new meaning and adds to your wealth.
Unlike mere money, it will enhance health.
For love makes life happy each day that you live.
And life is much richer when true love you give.

I WILL BE LISTENING

He said He was never far away,
that He could hear me if I called.
But I didn't need Him for that day
so I put off calling, hesitating and stalled.
The time slipped by and I floated on air,
never giving Him thought, never calling to mind
the fact that He was willing to share
all the heartaches and sorrows I left behind.
Soon I forgot to get in touch
for my life rolled on, happy, content.
I didn't need His comfort so much.
My memories of Him came and then went.
Life went on this way for a while
and then everything suddenly seemed to go wrong.
I didn't feel happy and I couldn't smile.
My heart didn't hear that happiness song.

Then I remembered the words of my Friend
and I felt so ashamed that tears freely fell.
I called out His Name and asked Him to send
the grace and forgiveness that would make me well.
"I will be listening," I heard His voice say.
"Tell me the problems that burden your heart.
"I'll give you strength sufficient each day.
"And leave you the peace that true love imparts."

At last I had found the Friend I had sought,
the One I had needed to guide me each day.
I knew with His blood my life had been bought.
Now in His Truth I was willing to stay.
"I will be listening." His words are like gold
in a world of foolishness filled with such pain.
I'll never forget them. They'll never grow old.
I've nothing to lose and Eternity to gain.

+ + +

"...Amen, amen, I say to you, if you ask the Father anything
in my name, He will give it to you."
John 16:23 KJV

BARNYARD GHOSTS

The chicken yard is silent,
the barn is strangely still.
The rooster no longer crows
upon the sunny hill.

The barnyard stands so empty,
the paddocks locked up tight.
Owls are the only visitors
near the barnyard late at night.

The building is weak and weathered,
its boards loose and rotten.
It speaks of a better time
that is now long forgotten.

The hay loft now is empty
and the barn door hangs askew;
a far cry from a better year
when it had all been new.

The golden dreams of yesterday
have long since come and gone.
The ghosts of children's laughter
haunt the shadows and linger on.

This was once a family haven
with its dreams and hopes and plans,
but time is the ultimate factor
in the works of mice and man.

+ + +

Empty dreams, empty hearts.

SEASON'S CHANGING SCENE

As the first leaves of autumn
turn to richest amber gold,
I know without a doubt
that soon it will be cold.

I shiver at the prospect
of the crisp, chilly air
and envision winters starkness,
the trees all stripped and bare.

I yearn so for the springtime
although winter is nigh at hand
for I shake and I shiver
as frosty weather takes command.

I'm not very fond of ice
nor am I pleased with snow.
I love the awakening season
when the earth begins to grow.

In the early morning sunlight
when the sun begins its climb,
I feel an urgency to hurry
for I know it will soon be time

to close up all the windows
and light the evening fire,
and stack the woodpile up
just a little higher.

And though season follows season,
one thing the cold will bring,
is the promise of renewal
with the new advent of spring.

THE RIGHT CHOICE

More and more you hear each day
of violence, sin and crime.
People tend to pass it off
as just the signs of the time.

And, yes, while these were long foretold
of things that had to be,
none of us would ever have thought
it would reach for you or me.

It would sadden the heart of an honest man
to think a loved one could be lost
in a maelstrom of violence or deadly crime
without first counting the cost.

What of a parent who tired of a life
of work without recompense,
who turned to crime to feed his child
losing all of his common sense?

And what of a child who wanted the world
right now and couldn't wait...
and turned to crime to gain the world,
then learned to deceive and hate?

And what of a world of deceit and lies
with mankind bent on corruption?
Governments fighting endless wars
rolling fast to the worlds destruction?

But wait!
There's a glimmer of light in this scene,
a *TRUTH* that could not be destroyed.
But one must reach for that Mighty Hand
if destruction he would avoid.

There really *is* an escape, an out,
if one will listen to that Voice...
but it's all up to you to learn and to do,
for it's *YOU* who must make that choice.

BE STILL

When the sun came up this morning
and it rose high in the sky,
the heart within me fluttered
for I instinctively knew why
that God created beauty
in the silence of the dawn
and it gave me strength to forge ahead
and steadily move along.

I remembered Gods sweet words
as He bid me to "Be still"
so I sat quietly listening
from my vantage on my hill.
I watched as nature awakened
and the animals moved about,
and it made my heart so joyful
that it wanted to jump right out.

It was hard to sit so quietly
just waiting for some sign
of a message from the heavens
from Jehovah's throne, divine.
But I learned in those still moments
that patience is a thing
that God rewards abundantly
and it makes a sad heart sing.

I can be undoubtedly truthful
when I say God gives rewards
to those who listen carefully
to His wise and loving words.
For He is our Grand Creator
and our Spiritual Father, too.
So if you are still and listening,
you will hear His blessings anew.

+ + +

"Be still, and know that I *am* God: I will be exalted
among the heathen, I will be exalted in the earth."
Psalm 46:10 KJV

APPRECIATION

I'm not as young as I used to be
nor as old as I'll be tomorrow,
but I'll not lament over trivial things
nor trouble my heart with sorrow.
I look for comfort in simple things
like flowers and birds and bees.
I like the sunshine on my face
and the shade beneath the trees.

I love the song of a babbling brook
for it calms my aching heart
and leaves a quietness in my soul
where love first got its start.
No, I'm not young but life is great
and I live each day as the last,
and I have only Jehovah to thank
for being my future, present and past.

THE LESSON

He came to the altar so brassy and bold,
demanding a solution for a problem of old.
He told God to take it right off of his hands
and wasn't so courteous with his forward demands.

Not once did he bow his head in quiet prayer
or acknowledge that Gods Spirit was even right there.
His knee did not bend nor hands clasp tight.
He felt his sharp words were duly his right.

He felt no peace, no sign of content.
The arrogance displayed he thought heaven-sent.
So he stood there expecting but no answer came.
Not once did he call God Almighty by Name.

The room was so silent, so empty and still.
Not once did he utter, "Oh, God, if You will."
So he turned away, dejected and sad.
He'd lost all the integrity that he'd ever had.

Oh, if only he'd prayed with sincerity contrite,
he'd have received affirmation that very same night.
But he missed his blessing; his joy did not grow.
God in His wisdom had plainly said "No".

God *always* hears prayers sincerely said
if we allow our spirits to be rightly led.
Be humble, not haughty, when we kneel to pray
and He'll grant us joy and peace for that day.

And if by chance His answer is slow,
then He might mean "wait" or maybe say "no".
But know that He hears you, no matter the need
and wants you to come to His prayer table to feed.

+ + +

"And when thou prayest, thou shalt not be as the hypocrites are:
for they love to pray standing in the synagogues and in the
corners of the streets, that they may be seen of men..."
Matthew 6:5 KJV

GIVE IT GAS

I was out of a job, no prospects in sight.
The rent was due on the following night.
I spent my last dollar on the paper that day.
Heaven only knew when I'd get my next pay.
I skimmed through the pages and there in bold print
were the words **"DRIVER WANTED"**...just what heaven sent.
I wasted no time and went and applied.
"Why, there's nothin'", I bragged, "in this world I've not tried."
As he put me in that bus behind that big wheel, I boasted loudly,
"This is gonna be a steal!"
I started the engine and pushed in the clutch
and shifted those gears with an experts touch.
One thing I didn't figure as I made my first mistake,
was the jerk and the squat when I pushed on the brake.
With a whirr and a jolt and escaping of air,
the engine sputtered loudly and conked out right there.
The thoughts in my mind I just let go past
as I heard the man tell me, "Give it gas. Give it gas!"

I practiced my driving till my shifting was neat,
coordinating perfectly my hands and my feet.
My stopping was easy, my take-off was smooth.
My C. D. L. license was now my next move.
I went through the inspection without any gig,
and then like a cowboy, I mounted my "rig."
With cock-sure confidence I turned on the key
while the testing officer kept her eagle eye on me.

The engine revved up a little too loud,
and I shoved it in gear so smugly and proud.
But I got my comeuppance and I sure could have cried,
for when I let the clutch out, the bus bucked and died.
I started that engine, fighting back tears,
'cause when I took off there was a grinding of gears.
I was sure that this test I never would pass
when the lady said scornfully, "Give it gas. Give it gas!"

Well, I got my license and landed the job.
Now my family savings I'd not have to rob.
I started my school route the very next day,
with great anticipation for my next pay.
I picked up the kids and soon learned their names
and quickly got wise to their discipline games.
The best fun I had was driving that bus,
but it made me so angry I wanted to cuss.
It bucked and it sputtered and ground on my nerves
and slowed to a crawl on hills and on curves.
But I reached my limit as I tried for a pass
when a five year old whispered, "Give it gas, man. Give it gas!"

"...and their soul shall be as a watered garden;
and they shall not sorrow any more at all."
Jeremiah 31:12b KJV

GARDEN OF LOVE

I planted unique seeds so fine
from Gods storehouse of love,
and Jehovah watered them lovingly
from His watershed high above.

I watched the sprouts of wisdom
grow a little bit each day
I cultivated and snipped them
and gave little cuttings away.

It was so amazing to see
those fragile cuttings grow.
I watered them with the Word of God
and their fruitage began to show.

Soon a garden so full of grace
basked in the love of God.
The seeds that I had planted
had been strengthened by His rod.

There wisdom and understanding
and knowledge began to grow;
all the precious flowers
that I had come to know.

I wanted others to share the joy
that I knew in my garden of love,
so I turned it back to the Master Gardener
Who smiles from heaven above.

+ + +

"He *is* green before the sun, and his branch
shooteth forth in his garden."
Job 9:16 KJV

"...A friend loveth at all times..."
Proverbs 17:17 KJV

FRIENDSHIP

Friendship is a special thing,
a *feeling* one imparts.
It's shared by trusting, caring souls
and linked with love from hearts.

Friendship can't be bought or sold.
It must be given with love.
It's a *gift* first given by Almighty God
Who sent it from heaven above.

WHAT WOULD JESUS DO?

What would Jesus do if
He lived in the world today?
Would He vote in the elections
or believe what the candidates say?

Would He make Himself popular
if He spoke against their views?
Would He welcome media coverage
or make the six o'clock evening news?

Would He expose their hearts so wicked
and invite a public debate?
Or would it cause an angry uproar
fueled with lies and open hate?

If Jesus lived here today
He'd likely step on peoples toes
with well placed words of wisdom
and love that grows and grows.

He'd show by His example
how to live a Christian life.
He'd bring peace to hearts long broken
in homes filled with strife.

He'd expose the rich man's folly
that money can buy all things.
He'd lighten the hearts of the burdened
until once more they would sing.

No more would there be sickness;
no doctor would earn a fee.
Christ's love would heal all illness
and He'd do it all for *free!*

He'd promote true love and brotherhood
and bring quality and equality too.
Just think about your decisions first,
then ask yourself...what would Jesus do?

SPRINGS PREVIEW

Silly little tulips, peeking from the ground.
Do they know something I don't know?
Or, do they stick their heads up just to look around
to see if there is yet a trace of snow?

Don't they know its winter and spring is long away?
Old man Frost has still a trick or two.
But those silly little tulip heads look like they're here to stay.
I wonder, if it snows, what they will do?

Perhaps they all got lonesome, so long beneath the ground,
and came up for a peek at Gods blue sky.
Then maybe they're a *preview* of spring's lovely sound,
gently pushing winters chill on by.

PRISONER'S?

They hung a "Welcome" sign out
but their house is locked up tight.
Their burglar alarm is set
against intruders in the night.

The dog lies by the doorstep,
his ears raised and alert,
ready to defend his household,
his aggressiveness to assert.

The motion detector is active
out by the locked back gate.
If anyone should dare enter,
surprise would seal his fate.

The phone sits on the nightstand,
the answering machine's near-by.
The monitors are in the kids rooms
listening for any cry.

Isn't it a bit ironic that in
this land of freedom and might,
we're locked up just like prisoners
for our protection every night?

+ + +

"And thou shalt be secure, because there is hope;
yea, thou shalt dig *about thee, and* thou shalt
take thy rest in safety.
Job 11:18 KJV

COMMON SENSE

If common sense was a commodity
that could be bought in a general store,
I wonder who would buy it
if it cost ten dollars or more?
Or if it was just a penny
or perhaps if it was free,
how many would take the offer
or walk by and let it be?

And if it was just for millionaires,
would they be standing in line
with caviar in one hand
and in the other a glass of wine?
Would common sense come in gold paper
and given only to the very elite?
Or would it be in plain brown wrapper
and black-marketed on the street?

If common sense was taught in the classroom,
would children be eager to learn,
or would they resist the efforts to teach them
and its wisdom they all would spurn.
If common sense was made of candy
or something else that was good to eat,
would it be sold in the grocery store
or hawked out on the street?

If common sense was a gift for royalty,
could common folks use it too?
If God made a choice between them,
would He give it to all or just a few?
If you were given the choice of a preference,
would your thoughts be muddled and dense?
Or would you use the brains God gave you
to rely on your good *common sense?*

LEAD ME, DEAR LORD

Use me wherever I am, Lord.
Teach me what I must do.
Show me the way that to You I must pray
so that I may be pleasing to You.

Tell me what I must say, Lord,
to turn even one sinner aside
from his evil ways for the rest of his days
and with You forever abide.

Lead me to the path I must follow
so that I may not stumble and fall.
Guide my feet aright in the darkness of night
so I'll not miss Your sweet loving call.

Teach me, Oh, Dear Lord and Savior,
so that I may abide in Your will.
Show me what to do as I look to You.
Through trial let me follow You still.

SAILORS AND DRAGONS

"The earth is flat," the ancients said
and gave the sailors much to dread.
But, out they sailed uncharted seas
for gold to seek and kings to please.

"Beware the dragons of the deep.
They rise by night and steal your sleep."
But, sail they did, out from the land
and put their trust in Gods Great Hand.

And fables told the ancients too,
for want of something more to do.
"The dragons eat the moon away.
They rise by night and feast by day."

With much to fear, the ancients fled
from foreign shores to freedom led.
And all the while the dragons, too,
sailed right behind on waters blue.

So many years have passed and more
while ancients rest on heavens shore.
The dragons, too, have passed away.
Or, do they hide in dreams today?

No matter now. The seas still flow
and sailors drift where oceans go.
Do they still see the dragons rise
where the earth is flat and meets the skies?

+ + +

"...And he shall slay the dragon that is in the sea."
Isaiah 27:1 KJV

JESUS CAME

He came to lead us back to God
by showing us His ways...
to make His Name known again
and giving Him the praise.

He came to show us how to live
in righteousness and love
and tell us of the Kingdom
He's establishing above.

He told us of the Rulership
that He has set apart
to guard and guide with loving ways
those with repentant hearts.

Oh, so much He gave to us.
His life He gladly laid
so we could gain eternal life...
the ultimate price He paid.

What can we give Him in return
for all His loving care,
but to follow in His footsteps now
and His righteous love to share.

THROW-AWAY AMERICA

They threw away their handkerchiefs
and threw away their cups.
They threw away their soft drink bottles, too.
They threw away their spray cans and threw away their towels.
Then they threw away the cans that held their brew.

They tossed away their morals for live-in love affairs.
They threw away their pride to foreign wars.
They blew away their president and his brother too,
and closed the channels to once friendly shores.

They wasted the resources that nature has to give,
and cluttered up the land with trashy things.
They air their dirty laundry in the eyesight of the world,
then sit back and get stepped on by oil kings.

They threw away their thinking with Mary-Jane and Angel Dust.
They dreamed with L. S. D. and mainline trips.
They threw away their chance at life with reds, blues and greens,
and little yellow pills on selfish lips.

Now they throw away their children in their foolish wanton lust.
The unborn die without a chance at life.
Will they throw away their freedoms and their faith in God as well
and surrender to the surgeons bloody knife?

Will they throw away their future without a second thought?
Will they not express their right to worship too?
Will they throw away religion and forget their sacred trust?
Without the help from God, *what will America do?*

JEHOVAH'S CHRISTMAS GIFT

In the hurry scurry of this day and age
you'll find that you're not on the same page
with others who also scurry about
so children won't have to do without
a Christmas gift on that special morn
when our Lord and Savior, Jesus was born.

We celebrate the birth of a child
who was born to a mother so meek and mild.
She bent to the will of the Father that day
and praised His Name as she knelt to pray.

God gave us a gift so precious and good,
Who stood in the place that no other man could...
a place of ridicule and sorrow,
so mankind could have a better tomorrow.

His gift so long ago that day
was the life of His Son to show us a way
to live in harmony, truth and love,
and guide us to heavenly places above.

No gift that we could give in return
could help us eternal life to earn.
No blood we could shed, no oath we declare
would assure us of a heavenly place up there.
The only gift acceptable above
is the act of repentance and a heart full of love.

So, why can't we all, this holiday season,
accept in our hearts that Christ is the reason
we may yet live in peace with one another
and call all men "Friend" and accept them as "brother".

For isn't that the real theme of the season...
and since Christ's birth is truly the reason...
Let us give thanks to Jehovah above
for the *gift* of His Son and His unfailing love.

Happy Birthday, Jesus!

HOSPITALS

Hospitals are lonely places.
The corridors are long and cold.
The antiseptic air is pungent.
The whispers are sad and old.

A young man paces the polished halls.
An old man slumps in his chair.
A patient is wheeled from surgery,
unaware that family is there.

A child whimpers in mothers arms
and is shushed and rocked to sleep.
Weariness etches a young girls face
while her long vigil she keeps.

The rustle of white starched uniforms,
the smiles and comforting tones
are food for the ailing spirit
and balm for the aching bones.

Prayers are whispered in heartfelt pain.
The waiting is endless as time.
The moon steals into the darkened sky
like a bright, new silver dime.

The squishing of shoes, a nod, a smile,
good news, dad's on his way back.
A 'thank you' is whispered in relieved sigh.
The tension of night shows a crack.

Silent prayers are quickly breathed.
Lines pull on tired faces.
One last glance down the long corridor…
hospitals are lonely places.

GODS QUESTIONS

Will you love Me in turmoil and pain
as you do in prosperity, joy and gain?
Will I be your God when things go wrong?
Will you still sing of your love in a song?

Will you still love Me when friends turn aside,
when problems attack you and you've no place to hide?
When those you love turn in despair?
When you reach for comfort and no one is there?

Will you call out My Name in the darkness of night,
fight against Satan and do what is right?
Will you look into My eyes on that Great Judgment Day?
If I ask, 'Do you love me?' what will you say?

GRANNY'S CHURN

Grandpa made the dasher from the handle of a broom.
The churn was accorded honor in the corner of the room.
It stood there in its silence awaiting the skillful hand
to whip it into action when some butter was in demand.

Granny added old Bessie's cream, so thick and rich and white,
then put the dasher in and fit the lid just right.
She sat in the straight chair and plunged the dasher up and down
as she set to singing songs with a rhythmic boogie sound.

Her feet tapped out the rhythm as a smile spread over her face.
It was like she was in dreamland, a different time, different place.
Sometimes when fretting babies were held on Granny's knee,
they were bounced to Granny's churning and soon they laughed with
glee.

Sometimes the cream made butter, it seemed in no time at all,
and Granny gave us buttermilk in glasses cold and tall.
But now and then the weather kept all us kids inside,
and when we'd get to fighting, there was no place to hide

from the stern hand of our Granny, so she made us take our turn
at plunging up and down that sturdy dasher in her churn.
Now there's nothing quite so humbling than a look from Granny's eye
that tells you you're in trouble and you soon would know just why,

for she handed you the dasher and pointed to the chair.
It was better than a "whuppin'" and you could see results right there.
Time has gone and so has Granny, and someday we'll take our turn.
But for now in my kitchen corner sets sweet memories and Granny's
churn.

+ + +

For my grandmother Ella Mae Holden Pell, with gratitude for
the churn given to me by my mother, Edith, her eldest child.

I WANT TO BELIEVE

She said that she would write to me,
to tell me all the news.
She said she'd call me now and then
and she smiled with her baby blues.

Oh, I want to believe she still remembers
the fun times that we had.
I want to believe but time goes by
and her absence makes me sad.

The mailman forgot to bring her letter.
I guess it slipped his mind.
But I'll look again, deeper in the box.
Maybe her letter I'll yet find.

I want to believe she'll send the pictures
she promised to send before
so I, too, can brag on my grandchild
and have memories left to store.

Perhaps she'll call on the telephone
and her sweet voice will cheer my heart.
And for just a few short moments
I'll forget we're so far apart.

I want to believe she hasn't forgotten
how to dial the telephone,
for since she left so long ago,
I sometimes feel so alone.

She's such a dear little grandchild
and I've enjoyed watching her grow.
The depth of love I have for her,
she may never really know.

I know the mind tends to forget
when they go so far away.
But still I ask God to protect her
when I kneel at night to pray.

I hope that time will not produce
a heart that may deceive.
Perhaps she gets too busy to remember.
She loves me. I *want* to believe.

JEHOVAH'S DIVERSITY

Everyone's different...
it's plain to see...
that our God, Jehovah
likes diversity.

If all men looked alike
and the women did too,
life would be so boring
for me and for you.

The babies that were born
would look like every other...
they'd grow up just the same
as their father or their mother.

The world would be confusing
if all houses built were square,
and you went to bed at night
to find a girl just like you there.

If the trees and vegetation
looked the same in every city,
they soon would be abandoned
and wouldn't that be a pity?

Now, isn't it a blessing
that God chose to *shake the tree*
and make us all look different
with our own personality?

TIME AND CIRCUMSTANCE

Though circumstances befall you
and time is near its end,
you need never be alone,
for Jehovah is your Friend.

Jesus stands beside you
to guard and guide your way.
He will give you comfort
when darkness hides the day.

Reach out to Him for guidance,
make requests in prayer.
He will always hear you.
In sorrows, He'll be there.

Speak to Him with confidence
and never doubt His plan,
for when the darkness threatens,
He will hold your hand.

+ + +

"For whosoever shall call upon the
name of the Lord shall be saved."
Romans 10:13 KJV

METAMORPHOSIS

When the winter wind comes whipping
around my window pane
and the storm clouds are threatening
to empty themselves of rain,
then my heart beats wild with wonder
as the lightning splits the sky
and I enjoy the noise of nature
until the maelstrom passes by.

Once the calm returns the beauty
of the early spring-like day,
my heart is also peaceful
as I bow my head to pray.
The air is fresh and wholesome
as the darkness then descends
and the many songs of nature
gradually slows and then ends.

The cares of the morrow
are futuristic still
as the last rays of light
fade beyond the farthest hill.
And the peace of the moment
is savored at long last
as the night morphs into morning
and the present becomes the past.

MY DREAMS

There was a time I had my dreams...
so many years ago.
And how I longed to see their fruits,
no one will ever know.
But time can change a lot of things
and dreams are shoved aside.
Reality always takes a seat
beside your dreams to ride.

Now and then the dreams return
for just a little while.
Creative juices start to flow
and evoke a remembered smile
of satisfaction for a work
that once was lost in time;
that once again comes to the fore,
be it prose, haiku, or rhyme.

I've had my dreams down through the years
and sometimes I still do.
And so I write of wondrous things,
of fantasy and of true.
Upon the clouds my dreams do fly.
That's all they are, it seems.
Life is too real to be ignored.
That's all they are...my dreams.

GOD'S PROMISES

You promised me light in the darkness.
You promised me warmth in the cold.
You promised me comfort in sorrow
   and help when I am grown old.

You said You'd be with me in trouble,
that strength in travail You'd provide.
And when my enemies surround me,
   You'd give me a safe place to hide.

I know You'll remember Your promises,
   for You are the true God alone.
Whatever You say You'll accomplish.
You claim the faithful as Your Own.

Oh, help me the straight path to follow,
   that I may not err on the way.
Grant me Your grace and forgiveness,
   to live for Your glory each day.

WHAT COLOR IS LOVE?

A little girl sat drawing
with crayons on a pad.
Her dark eyes looked puzzled
at the picture that she had.
She had colored almost all of it,
then put her crayons down.
She stared at the unfinished picture
and her smile turned to a frown.
"I've colored all of it," she said,
"except this tiny bit.
"And I can't make up my mind
"just what color to make it.
"What color is *love*, Mama?"
she asked in sweet concern.
I decided then and there
that it was something we both should learn.
"Blue is the color of the sky," I said,
"And love is sometimes blue.
"Love is bright and sunny,
"so love is yellow, too.
"Love is often festive,
"so orange could be just right.
"And sometimes love brings sadness,
"so it can be black as night.

"You know, love can be jealous,
"so green is the color to use.
"And love can also be hurtful,
"so brown is the one to choose.
"Red is the color of blood
"and also a beautiful rose.
"But the real color of love,
"only your heart really knows."
She picked up the crayons,
a smile playing on her face,
and she filled the paper with color
where there was empty space.
She held it up so proudly
and I wept to finally know
that the true color of love
was like God's heavenly rainbow.

FAITH AND BELIEF

We cannot see beyond the bend,
but God is always there.
He knows the beginning from the end.
He keeps you in His care.

Faith will always see you through
the trials that come your way,
so to persevere is the thing to do
and *believe* in what you *pray.*

For Bill H.

+ + +

"For with the heart one exercises faith for
righteousness, but with the mouth one makes
public declaration for salvation.
For the Scripture says: "None that rests his faith
on him will be disappointed."
Romans 10:10, 11 NWT

I SEE A GARDEN

I see a garden.
True, the ground is bare
of what used to be.
It's quite different now.
There's not much to see.
But, though the ground is bare,
Nature's phantoms are still there,
leaving remnants of beauty for me.

I see a garden.
There are cabbages in a row
on that far side.
The vines on that trellis
give the cukes a place to hide.
The birds all seem to know
where the ripening strawberries grow
and the weeds grow thickest on that side.

I see a garden.
Though traces of snow cover
the sleeping seeds of spring,
there is life beneath the soil
and new birth the sun will bring.
Though old age may hinder me
and I'm not what I used to be,
I see a garden in my heart
and *my soul SINGS!*

ENCOURAGING WORDS

Satan comes in many forms,
God's children to deceive,
to draw away the sons of God
and hurt those who believe.
He comes in guises of delight
to tempt the human heart
and entice it from the hand of God
so from Him they'll soon depart.

"Be sly as the fox and meek as the lamb"
is God's wise admonition.
Don't give Satan an upper hand
or furnish him ammunition.
Just hang on to the Word of God,
for in Him is your delight.
Remember there is no One like Him.
He is your *Arm of Might.*

He cares for you through all of life's storms,
no matter your stage in life.
He'll see you through and be your strength,
whatever your sin or strife.
So fight the good fight day and night.
Don't yield to Satan's whim.
He'll drag you to despairing depths
and make you just like him.

You'll be forever lost to God
if Satan's companion you'll be.
He will enslave you to himself
and you'll never again be free.
Heed the Word of God today.
Give God your allegiance and love.
Your reward will be happiness, joy unending
and a home in heaven above.

AMAZING LOVE

There is Someone Who loves me,
Someone I cannot see,
Who allows me choice and freedom
to be what I want to be.
He does not criticize me
when I falter or I fail.
He extends His hand to help me
so in sin I do not flail.
He greets me every morning
with the sunshine of His smile.
And if the day dawns dreary,
He bids me wait a little while.
He grants me strength in weakness
when temptation looms my way.
And in my shame and sorrow
He prompts my heart to pray.
I know I'm far from perfect,
yet He watches from above
and touches me with the perfection
of His amazing love.

DADDY'S LEARNED DAUGHTER

Daddy taught it to my brothers.
He taught it to my son.
And I watched so I would know
just what has to be done.

Check the wires and spark plugs.
Make sure that they all fire.
Look at the electrical system.
Replace any frayed wire.

Check the carburetor
to see the fuel comes through
and change the PCV valve
and the fuel filter too.

Replace the old air filter
so the air intake is clean.
And don't forget the points
just because they can't be seen.

Make sure the distributor cap
isn't cracked and fits up tight.
The engine is pretty old
but it's always run just right.

Check all the reservoirs
to be sure they're filled right up.
And don't forget the fluid
in the brake cylinder cup.

Change the oil and filter
and lube all the joints.
Daddy always told me not
to forget these finer points.

Test the brakes and cylinders
and pack the bearing too.
Rotate the tires and balance them
and align the front end too.

Replace the wiper blades
and then test the lights.
Winter's almost here
and there's long, dark, cold nights.

And don't forget the heater.
It's got to keep me warm.
I don't want the air conditioner
to come on in a winter storm.

Now, don't get all aflutter.
It might cause your toes to curl.
Daddy only taught the boys these things.
After all, *I'm just a girl!*

YOUR TREASURES

What treasures do you go out to find
in this day of age and space?
Do you find the treasures that you seek
puts you in the biggest race
to acquire so many material things and then as life goes by,
you view your progress with critical eyes
and begin to wonder "why"
you struggled so hard for material gain,
for that's what you thought you were worth.
Did you know God valued you more from before
your conception or even your birth?
So what treasures do you go out to find?
Is it spiritual you seek to gain?
With what do you endeavor to fill your mind?
Is it pleasurable to cause others pain?
What treasures do you wish to leave behind
when your life expires at last,
and you realize you can't take it with you
and you must leave it in the past.
Would it not have been better for your treasures to be
of the more spiritual kind?
For then they'd surely be waiting for you
when you leave this old world behind.

+ + +

"Stop storing up for yourselves treasures upon the earth,
where moth and rust consume, and where thieves break in and steal.
Rather, store up for yourselves treasures in heaven,
where neither moth nor rust consumes, and where thieves
do not break in and steal. For where your treasure is,
there your heart will be also."
Matthew 6:19-21 NWT

73

APPEARANCE & PREJUDICES

Jesus was a Jewish man; the Bible tells us so.
This fact raises questions...the answers I want to know.
If Jesus' eyes were slanted and his skin a golden hue,
would people then have welcomed Him and all that He would do?
And what if He was big and fat with a waddle in His walk?
Suppose He had a distinctive lisp or stutter in His talk?
Would people be apt to listen then or laugh Him on to scorn?
Would Jesus have cursed the circumstances under which He had been
born?
What if His lips were heavy and thick and His nose large and flat?
Would people have listened to Him then if our Savior looked like
that?
Suppose His hair was kinky and His skin tone black as night?
Would that have made a difference to the man He gave back sight?
If He had come as a full grown man with skin as red as wine,
with jet black hair and eyes like coal, would He have been more di-
vine?
Would man have heeded His words because of the skin He bore
or be as prejudicial then because of the clothes He wore?
If Jesus came back here today, would people realize
that He was the Savior, Son of God, by the shape and hue of his eyes?
And if He chose to be bold and brassy, with a language peppery and
hot,
would man then give Him proper due or cast Him the very same lot?

Would He have bled less being shorter, or if His skin was white?
What if He had a balding head, would that have made Him all right?
Would our sins have been less heavier and the burden less to bare
if Jesus wore a nose ring, pierced His navel or dyed His hair?
The way man judges others cannot give honor and due,
for but by the mercy and grace of God, there could have been me or
you!

+ + +

"Judge not, that ye be not judged. For with what judgment ye judge,
ye shall be judged: and with what measure ye mete, it shall be
measured to you again."
Matthew 7:1, 2 KJV

FOR YOU, LORD

This is for You, Lord.
It's not about me.
I know I'm not worthy of thought.
But I will still sing
my praises to Thee
and give honor just as I ought.
You are the Master, Creator of all.
The Owner of all You survey.
Take this world in hand
and shake it up
and teach mankind how to obey.
No one deserves honor and praises but You.
You were the First One to love.
You have the right to be
Sovereign and King
on earth and in heaven above.

+ + +

"Look unto me, and be ye saved, all the ends of the earth:
for I *am* God, and *there is* none else.
I have sworn by myself, the word is gone out of my mouth
in righteousness, and shall not return, That unto me every knee
shall bow, every tongue shall swear."
Isaiah 45:22, 23 KJV

BUS DRIVERS LAMENT

I was sitting at a stop light
in my brand new Am Tran bus,
when my stomach started cramping
and my gut began to fuss.
Then I had a familiar feeling
and I hoped that it would pass,
for I didn't want my students
to know that I had gas!

Now, I knew some exercises,
or so, I've been told,
that can strengthen certain muscles
when Nature declares you're getting "old."
So I squeezed my hips together
and drew in a cleansing breath
in an effort to be self-controlled
and not embarrass myself to death.

With the stop light changing color
the traffic began to flow,
so I carefully accelerated
and the bus was good-to-go.
The kids got a little louder
as my engine wound on out.
I hoped they wouldn't notice
that I strangely squirmed about.

I began to feel more confident
as I squeezed and breathed just right,
but it wasn't very long before
I knew I'd lost the fight,
for as hard as I tried to control myself,
I suddenly had to sneeze.
Then a little boy behind me yelled,
"Whew! Who cut the cheese!"

To say that I was mortified
would not be quite true,
but under the circumstances,
really, what could I do?
So I opened up the window
and in the rear view gave a glare,
then shook my head disapprovingly
at some boys innocent stare.

It seemed he saw right through me,
and I felt my face grow red,
but I had to keep things under control
and not lose my head.
"You should at least say 'excuse me',"
I said in mock expression.
I vowed never to eat beans for lunch,
for I think I learned my lesson!

BE BOLD

Don't be ashamed to talk about Jesus.
Don't be embarrassed to speak God's Name.
Don't be afraid of what others think.
It's not a story...it's not a game.

Don't hesitate to tell Jesus' story
of His perfect life, His wonderful love.
If you're ashamed to tell about Jesus,
He'll be ashamed to defend you above.

Speak sweet words of exaltation.
Lift His Name each time you do.
Great rewards not yet known
will be your own, will come to you.

Be straight forward, brave and bold
when you speak Jesus' Name in love.
He will speak your name to Jehovah
when you stand before God's throne above.

+ + +

"For whosoever shall be ashamed of me and of my words,
of him shall the Son of man be ashamed, when he shall come
in his own glory, and *in his* Father's, and of the holy angels."
Luke 9:26 KJV

GOD'S FRIEND

He's not so comely-featured
but he's got deep blue-gray eyes
that evoke a sense of compassion,
that seem young, yet old and wise.

His hands are large and gnarly
from the work he does each day,
but they transform into cotton
when he folds them together to pray.

His voice is strong and assertive
when he speaks God's Name in love.
I can imagine the angels smiling
as they carry his praises above.

Oh, he makes such beautiful music
when he composes a spiritual song.
I find myself humming the tune
while I work the whole day long.

He speaks no words of eloquence.
His words are simple and plain.
They hide the beauty of his soul
and conceal his deep-felt pain.

Only those that love him
can see and comprehend
why God has called and chosen
him to be His "special friend."

+ + +

For Uncle Windell, Jehovah's friend.

WAR-TORN WORLD

In the midst of war and turmoil,
in the sounds of battle cries,
I look up and see the gun smoke
meld with white clouds in the skies.
The bombs explode so loudly
and assault my weary ears.
The tortured land around me
tells the story of all my fears.

There's no rest in the darkness
when the sun in faith moves on
to the other side of the world
where peace dwells in early dawn.
But it brings no peace at daybreak
when its rays reach the earth.
Its rising begs an answer
to "What is war really worth?"

Is it worth the tortured landscape?
Is it worth the anguished cries
of the widows and the orphans
when their loved ones cruelly die?
It comes down to greed and money,
selfishness, oil and sin.
Every nation thinks they're right
and each one prays that they will win.

How can a god of righteousness
sanction terrible death and war,
where peace is just wishful thinking
and Christian love lives no more?
God does not forget the faithful
who bows head and bends the knee.
Even in a war-torn world
He will remember you and me.

+ + +

"In the world you are having tribulation; but take courage!
I have conquered the world."
John 16:33b NWT

THE ANCIENT WARRIOR

Sometimes I sit and listen
and I hear the mournful cry
of an ancient family warrior
from a time long since gone by.
I feel the pain within him
as his land all passed away
and his people slowly vanished
as he raised his hands to pray.

In the quiet of the evening
as the sun began to fade,
I heard voices in the wind
and they chanted as they prayed.
It was the ancient warriors
as our people once had been,
asking the Great Spirit Father
for protection way back then.

In the wind the voices carried
from an era long ago,
the prayers of their thanksgiving
with words I seemed to know.
I stood transfixed and listening
while the tears slipped from my eyes,
for I understood the mourning
in the warriors prayerful cries.

The last sunrays then faded
past the pine trees on the hill.
The warrior's song was silenced
but I could feel him still.
For my heart has stirred a memory,
though it was not my own,
of a time when there was freedom
such as I have never known.

In the quiet of the evening
as the stars began to shine,
my heart touched an ancient warriors
and made that memory mine.

JESUS' WORD

He said I would be persecuted
by the ones I love.
He said that He would strengthen me
if I would look above.

He promised He would comfort me
with love that has no end.
And if I should call out His Name,
on Him I could depend.

I have found His Word is true,
though oft' I go astray.
It's then I ask Him to forgive
when humbly I kneel and pray.

JUVENILES

They're just like bantam roosters,
young cockerels at play,
in search of many conquests
each and every day.
They challenge and they side-step
like dancers on a stage.
They thrust at life, then parry
in fits of violent rage.

They cannot seem to conquer
the spirit jailed inside,
never giving one iota.
They're just along for the ride.
There is no communication.
They grunt, pass gas and groan.
You might trust them with your life,
but don't leave them home alone.

You can't give them words of wisdom
for they already know it all.
You just have to be there for them
to pick them up when they fall.
If they could skip from 10 to 20
and forgo the painful years,
it would save a lot of heartache,
growing pains and bitter tears.

You never know what they're thinking.
If you ask, they will not tell,
but they'll confide in each other,
even someone they don't know well.
Before you close your eyes at night
you pray for strength from above,
to guard and guide these young children
for they were gifts through God's great love.

A BEGGAR

I am a beggar of many things,
of bright sunny skies and birds that sing.
I ask for warmth on a cold fall morn,
and the chance to see new life be born.
I ask for water when thirst overtakes,
and I beg forgiveness for foolish mistakes.
I ask for health when illness looms nigh.
I ask for peace when my heart wants to cry.
I ask for a kinder, more tolerant heart,
where compassion and understanding must start.
And I ask for knowledge for what I don't know
and wisdom to plant seeds of knowledge to grow.
I ask for the freedom to worship the Lord
and the courage to speak the Truth of His Word.
I beg for the fire that burns deep within
and a humble heart forgiven of sin.
I ask for strength when my spirit is weak,
and a spark in the darkness as His light I seek.
Yes, a beggar I am, and a beggar I'll be,
for He begged of His Father pardon for me.

+ + +

"And I say unto you, Ask, and it shall be given you;
seek, and ye shall find; knock, and it shall be opened unto you.
For every one that asketh receiveth; and he that seeketh findeth;
and to him that knocketh it shall be opened."
Luke 11:9, 10 KJV

CHILDHOOD FANTASIES

We used to lie in bed at night
and tell each other tales
of ghosts and goblins in the dark
and ships with billowing sails.
We'd scare each other to the point
we'd fear to go to sleep.
And then we'd say our prayers and ask
the Lord us safely to keep.
We'd listen to the creaking stairs
and it gave us such a fright
to imagine ghostly figures coming
to get us in the night.
We covered our heads to try and hide,
hoping no one could see.
We imagined ourselves invisible then
so the goblins would let us be.
We'd sleep up close for comfort
so we would not feel alone
because we scared ourselves so much
with ghost stories of our own.
But soon our fears began to fade
and our eyes closed in sleep.
Our sisterly love kept us close and warm
while God's angels their vigils did keep.

+ + +

For my two sisters, Ivagene and Barbara,
my childhood companions, my sisters of love.

GIFT OF LOVE

Through all the storms of life
I have loved You.
I called Your Name when
no one else was there.
And if the day was dark
and held contention,
I could but speak Your Name
to know You cared.

In moments of pure joy
with heart high soaring,
I burst with love and
called Your Name anew.
I had to share this gift
of exaltation,
because my heart told me
it came from You.

+ + +

"And you will actually seek me and find (me)",
for you will search for me with all your heart."
Jeremiah 29:13 NWT

ANGELS UNAWARE

God sends us angels
when we are least aware,
to guide us in our troubles
and give us special care.
We don't always know the reason
strangers stop and help us out,
but we'd like to believe that "love your neighbor"
is what it's all about.

You can talk until you're breathless
but it's "action" that's the key
that will bring about solutions
helpful both to you and me.
Heaven knows when help is needed
so God sends the angels then
to lead us through the roadblocks
and guide us back again.

Each day look for the angels
that shine from strangers faces.
You may meet them any moment
in the most unusual places.
So be certain they are near you,
any place and anywhere.
You'll never know it but you could be
meeting *angels unaware*.

+ + +

"Let brotherly love continue.
"Be not forgetful to entertain strangers: for
thereby some have entertained angels unawares."
Hebrews 13: 1, 2 KJV

COUNT THE RAINBOWS

Count the rainbows in each day
and not the storms of life.
God will always help you deal
with pain and daily strife.
Rainbows often can be seen
after a summer storm
to remind us of God's promises
to keep us safe from harm.

If our storms come frequently,
don't fret nor be dismayed.
Sometimes our rainbows teach us patience
when they are delayed.
Some storms come up suddenly
when you least expect them to.
Prayer and supplication
is all that you can do.

Sometimes we have to wait a while,
for God's time is not ours.
We must remember rainbows
follow those summer showers.
So turn your eyes toward heaven
and search the skies above.
God will send you comfort
in the rainbows of His love.

+ + +

"I do set my bow in the cloud..."
Genesis 9:13a KJV

APPRECIATION

Lord, I love the sunshine
filtering through the trees.
And, Lord, I love the morning air
rustling the autumn leaves.
Lord, I love the dew drops
so crystal clear and bright,
and the way You place them on the grass,
every one just right.

You really are the Artist,
Your talent infinitely best.
None can be Your equal
no matter time or test.
So, I'll just say "I love You"
with humble heart contrite,
trusting that You'll hear me
and that my words are right.

+ + +

*"Jesus said unto him, 'Thou shalt love
the LORD thy God with all thy heart,
and with all thy soul, and with all thy
mind. This is the first and great
commandment."*
Matthew 22:37, 38 KJV

MESSAGE ON A BRIDGE

I saw an old covered bridge today
and walked beneath its dome.
It gave me a feeling of protectiveness
such as that of hearth and home.
Below the bridge rushed water.
I could hear its babbling song
as it hurried toward the ocean,
never resting all the day long.

The breeze blew through the old archway,
its touch so cool and clean.
It gave me a comforting feeling
and a sense of beauty unseen.
It wasn't a beauty for eyesight,
but one that's seen within,
a beauty felt in the heart-wall,
like the touch of a beloved friend.

The shadows were dark and inviting
so I investigated each one,
and found nothing in the shadows
that was not present beneath the sun.
The walls held countless carvings
of initials, dates and names,
and one part was dark and scorched
as if it had been licked by flames.

I read all the love notes and scribbles
and I smiled as most would do,
until I read in tortured scrawling,
"whoever reads this, I love you."
Suddenly old memories came flooding
and I recalled a young child in despair,
who had come to the bridge at twilight
and scribbled through tears with great care.

It was hard to read more for my teardrops
made it almost impossible to see.
The words ate at my heartstrings,
for the child who had written them was me.

I THINK OF YOU

The many years we've spent together,
really more than half my life,
serves to prove how much I've loved you,
more than when I became your wife.
So many memories flash before me
of the inexperienced eager bride
who knew nothing of being a wife and mother,
and who's ignorance was really hard to hide.

In my moments of revelry,
when thoughts of you crowd in tight,
I think of you way back then
and dream my dreams in the night.
I think of you and wonder then,
if circumstances were different too,
if we'd be here together now,
or if we'd grown apart like some do.

I think of you and how you've changed.
I know I'm not the same as then.
But, I do wonder where I'd be
if I had walked a different road back when...
back when my life was young and full...
back when the children were not there.
Back when life was fresh and new
and I had no one to love and care.

I think of you and wonder why
you stood beside me all the while
our kids were growing to adulthood.
I think of you and then I smile.

+ + +

For Charles, the man I love, the man I married.

96

SPRING HOPE

Beneath the ice and snow today
I came upon a scene
that made my heart jump with joy.
It was a speck of green.

This winter long, so cold and white,
when everything was bare,
I felt depressed, asleep inside,
without a hope, without a care.

But, then today a hope was born
and darkness soon began to pass,
and all because beneath the snow
peeked a single blade of grass.

CHANGED

What can I do for You, Lord?
You've done so much for me.
You've taken the scales from my worldly eyes
so that I can plainly see
that I've been less than sinless.
I've wallowed in worldly ways.
I've stirred the pot of discontent
and darkened Your sunshine rays.

But, You took my heart of darkness
and cleaned it bright and new.
You changed my hate to purest love
and planted seeds that grew.
You made me see my errors.
I've changed and have become new.
Now, my sweet Lord Jesus,
what can I do for You?

+ + +

"Therefore if any man be in Christ, he is a new
creature: old things are passed away; behold,
all things are become new."
II Corinthians 5:17 KJV

CONTEMPLATION

I contemplated my thumb today.
I stared at it a long while.
I looked at all its wrinkles and lines
and thought I detected a smile.

I viewed all its nooks and crannies
as I turned it this way and that.
I thought it resembled a wizened old man
without his black bowler hat.

I noticed the half-moon on its nail
with cracks and splits on the end.
I saw the knot on the misshapen knuckle
and the way it struggled to bend.

Then I thought how wonderful a thumb must be
to accompany a finger to grasp,
much like the marriage of a hook and eye,
or the locking part of a hasp.

Now, you might think it strange of me
and consider an appendage quite dumb.
But, I'd rather give praise to a wonderful Creator
Who had the foresight to give me a thumb.

+ + +

"I shall laud you because in a fear-inspiring way I
am wonderfully made. Your works are wonderful,
as my soul is very well aware.
"My bones were not hidden from you.
"Your eyes saw even the embryo of me, and in your
book all its parts were down in writing, as regards
the days when they were formed..."
Psalms 139:14, 15a, 16a, b.   NWT

BALTIMORE'S CHILD

She sat there on the sidewalk,
hot tears streaked down her face,
with a sadness in her eyes
that time would not erase.

Her clothes were worn and tattered.
No shoes adorned her feet.
Her hair was all disheveled.
She was a picture of defeat.

Hunger was her constant companion
that seldom left her side.
She slept in cardboard boxes
to keep warm and play and hide.

There were many days of sorrow
and a few where laughter fared.
Some were filled with sunshine
when a stranger some kindness shared.

She dreamed of home and family
that she might have some day,
and of a scented backyard garden
where her friends could come to play.

It doesn't matter skin color.
Poverty has no hue or tone.
Hunger harbors no prejudice,
nor does being all alone.

She's an orphan of the ages,
so young, yet she's always been.
She's innocent of life's harsh burdens,
faultless, yet born into sin.

She's a prodigy of the inner city,
a product of society gone wild.
She reflects a timeless profession.
She's Destiny...Baltimore's Child.

HELP IS JUST A PRAYER AWAY

Don't let depression run your life,
don't give way to despair.
Remember behind the clouds of gloom
the sun is shining there.

Behind a frown there lies a smile,
and laughter cheers the heart.
Just reach way down and pull it out
and watch a chuckle start.

Old Satan loves to roam at night
where darkness fills the air.
So if your candle does not flicker,
he'll fill that space in there.

Don't let him win! Don't let him in
a heart that's pure and true,
for help is just a prayer away,
if you let God's love shine through.

+ + +

"A merry heart doeth good *like* a medicine:
but a broken spirit drieth the bones."
Proverbs 17:22 KJV

MY OLD BUS

The bus brakes squeal, the lights are growing dim.
The seats are a little worn and so is the leather trim.
The yellow paint's grown dull and no longer takes a shine,
but that old bus is dependable. It runs and it's mine.

The old heater's broken. In the mornings it's quite cold.
The ride is really bouncy 'cause the springs are pretty old.
The steering needs tightening. There's play in the wheel.
The oil pan leaks 'cause there's a break in the seal.

And I have to add oil nearly every other day.
You could follow my route 'cause the drip shows the way.
The engine won't idle till the anti-freeze is warm.
The roof leaks like a sieve from the least little storm.

The tires all need replacing. They've got patches everywhere.
I tell myself daily that it's just wear and tear.
It jiggles and it rattles but the kids don't make a fuss,
'cause they know they'd have to walk if it weren't for my old bus.

+ + +

In fond memory of old S-2.

RAPERS OF THE FOREST

One day they came, these rapers,
with their saws and big machines.
And I heard the groan of the forest
and the felled woods silent screams.

The thud of the falling giants
in the last throes of their lives
cut my own heart to pieces
as if with many sharpened knives.

Farewell, my shady companions.
You and I have lived as one,
side by side these many years
with the rising and setting sun.

Farewell, my friends, the woodland,
home to the lives within.
My heart cries for your departure,
for the comfort you've always been.

Alas, the world is changing,
for the rapers have had their day.
The giants lay dead and barren,
no longer can the forest stay.

The rains will now cause erosion.
The wildlife will have no home.
And I, like the Ancients before me,
will soon fade and go on alone.

+ + +

"For everything there is an appointed time,
even a time for every affair under the heavens:
a time for birth and a time to die; a time to plant
and a time to uproot what was planted; a time to kill
and a time to heal; a time to break down and a time
to build;..."
Ecclesiastes 3:1-3 NWT

THE HUNTER

He rose before the early dawn.
Excitement filled his heart.
Today was his initiation and
the hunt was about to start.

He grabbed his bow and quiver
filled with arrows sharp and true.
His father had taught him well
and he knew what he must do.

Swiftly and so stealthily
he crept out of the camp
and made his way to the woodland edge
through grasses tall and damp.

The muscles of his legs were taut
as he crept on through the trees.
His fingers twitched as he held the bow.
There was quivering in his knees.

In great anticipation
he dreamed of his first kill.
His father had taught him to rely
upon his wit and skill.

All around were sounds of life.
Birds called high in the trees.
Steps of furry animals
mixed with buzzing of the bees.

He came into a clearing
and there before him stood
a great majestic creature
just inside the shadowy wood.

Slowly, oh, so slowly,
he put arrow to the bow
and brought it up so gradually
that his movement didn't show.

He fixed onto his target
but his hands began to shake.
It was then he realized how
much courage it would take.

He lowered the bow slightly
so to get a better aim,
but he didn't like the feeling
of revulsion that somehow came.

The suspense of the moment
was almost too much to bear
as he sighted down his arrow
at the creature standing there.

And then at just that instant
the creature looked him in the eye.
He lowered his trembling hands,
though he didn't quite know why.

He had missed the perfect moment
but strangely, he didn't care
that he hadn't shot his arrow
at the creature standing there.

He stood so still and silent
as the deer turned slowly away,
and he felt only relief
that he hadn't killed it today.

The silence was overpowering,
as was the absence of fear.
On his face was the look of pride,
and the stain of a single tear.

+ + +

For all of Jehovah's magnificent creatures.

ALABAMA'S HILLS

Born in the hills of Alabama,
in a log cabin amidst the pines,
above a river running swiftly,
where the whispering breezes whine.

I walked the forest of pine needles
and sought its treasures wild and free.
It was for me a secret haven
shared by others just like me.

I often thought I saw a figure
in the shadows crouching low.
It may have been just wishful dreaming
of my kinsfolk long ago.

Someday I'll go back to that yonder
where life was sweet and time was still.
I'll wander through the great pine forest
and be home again in Alabama hills.

I long for peace amidst the woodland
and from which I'd ne'er more roam.
I'd gladly go back to that haven,
back to my Alabama home.

THE SHOE THAT FITS

There's always someone who'll disagree
with any phase of philosophy.
Regardless of place, disrespecting the hour,
he can be seen in his ivory tower
loudly protesting one thing or another,
agreeing neither with mankind nor brother.
But just let him be in want for himself,
watch him quickly jump off his shelf
of self-importance, as he takes the lead,
for now it is *he* who has the need.

Now don't take offense at this altruism
for it's not meant to be criticism
of words or feelings thrown in your direction,
so you should not feel the need for protection.
But, if you feel pinched a bit here and there
or feel the heat of a probing stare,
just take a moment to ponder, then air it.
For if the "shoe fits," then by all means...
WEAR IT!

THANKSGIVING AND LOVE

I think of You so often,
throughout my busy day
and ask Your help continually
as for more strength I pray.

And it's with humble gratitude
my heart is filled with love,
for I know You will answer
from Your great throne far above.

Each day of life You grant me
brings new joys and blessings too,
so it's with my love unending
my thanks I give to You.

+ + +

"O Give thanks unto the LORD, for He is good..."
Psalms 118:1a KJV

MY FOREVER FRIENDS

Today I passed a milestone,
a turning point in life.
I stand ready to face tomorrow
with its struggles, joy or strife.

Whatever the load I'm given,
I know Jesus will be right there
to comfort, guide, instruct me,
for I know I'm in His care.

I have friends who won't forsake me,
who will be there if I call.
Their hands will help and guide me
and pick me up if I should fall.

They've been handpicked by my Jesus.
Should I falter, I'll make amends.
My Savior knew what's best
when He gave me my *forever friends*.

+ + +

For all my bus driver friends, my contractors, my students
and their wonderful parents, and all the teachers and staff
of Bel Air Middle School, Emmorton Elementary School,
William S. James Elementary School, Heidi & Chris Peach,
and Howard Harper.
My heartfelt *THANKS!*

FALLS DELIGHT

The leaves! The leaves!
They look like snow,
whirling, twirling in the wind.
They hustle and bustle with a
rustling sound.
They dance the jig as they
bow and bend.

The wind! The wind!
It tickles and tosses
the leaves in rhythmic dance.
It pushes them under bushes
and around trees,
then it scatters them all askance.

The dance of the leaves
in a fall symphony
builds a crescendo of delight.
It excites the hearts of
nature lovers
as fall settles in for the night.

THE ROAD TO LOVE

It is not for us to judge,
for we are sinners, too.
Perhaps not in the things we say,
nor always what we do.

Our sin could be one of neglect
by ignoring those in need.
We may avert our guilty eyes
and to unfortunates pay no heed.

Our brother may be slowly drowning
in worldly, hurtful woe.
The pain and sorrow he endures,
we may never really know.

Just because our feet may be
on ground of solid stone,
does not mean we can walk by
and leave him sink alone.

Reach down, reach down, and take his hand
and pull him from the mire.
Give your brother a helping hand
and let him climb up higher.

Who knows? The course that we may take
will guide us to each other
and we'll be richer for having found
the way to love our brother.

CHESAPEAKE KING

True, he's just an old sea dog,
but he said to me one day,
"Do ye hear the sound of the breaking waves
as they dance across the bay?
They whisper along the eddies
and caress the rocky shore.
The song's the same sweet music as
it's been a thousand years or more.
Out yonder when the waves are choppy
and there's white caps standing high,
don't fear the thunderous roar 'cause
the light house is close by.
Its beacon is always burning,
searching the rolling sea.
And the fog horn in the darkness
turns a comfort inside of me."
Then he sucked on his old corncob
and blew a wreath above his head.
His glasses slipped down on his nose
and then to me he said,
"Out yonder, gal, in the darkness
'neath the veil of yaller light,
the stars shine down like diamonds
that cut into the night.

It's then I feel a sweetness that
stirs my salty heart.
And I know then, that Rosie and me's
been too long apart.
And I get a deep down yearning
to hold my Rosie tight
and feel her close to me
like the salty sea at night."
I catch a glimpse of mistiness
that settles in his eyes
and hear his old voice tell me
that a captain *never* cries.
But, this old salt's no captain
like one has ever seen.
He's just my sweet old grandpa,
and to me he's a *Chesapeake King!*

FOLLOW THE SON

When the days are long and dreary
and the winter has begun,
pack your bags, your comb and toothbrush,
grab your keys and *follow the sun.*

When your job begins to bore you,
and no accolades you've won,
clean your desk and clear your mind.
Say "so long" and *follow the sun.*

If life in general gives no peace,
and you're in tears when day is done,
get on your knees, spill out your heartache,
bow your head and *follow the Son!*

Follow the Son to untold glory.
He'll lift your burdens when life is done.
He'll cleanse your heart of every foible.
Yield your soul and *follow the Son!*

FUN WITH MY SISTERS

Butterflies in the summer,
crickets in the fall,
lightning bugs in the evenings...
I liked them most of all.
Kick the can and soft ball,
jump rope, Double Dutch,
Old Maid cards and checkers,
games we loved so much.
Cutting out paper dolls,
designing their dresses too.
Coloring in our coloring books
were things we liked to do.
Trading comics on our block
to read on rainy days.
Playing monopoly and pick-up-sticks
was fun in so many ways.
Walking together in the woods,
poke salad greens to find.
Crab apples and berries too
with sweet jellies in mind.
Stories in the night time
as in our beds we lay.
It was the best of endings
for an active fun-filled day.

Oh, the memories are so precious
of our childhood long ago
and they give me so much pleasure,
more than anyone could know.
My, but we loved one another,
though we fought as children do.
But we always stuck together
and we all grew closer too.
Years have not come between us.
Problems didn't pull us apart.
Time may have changed our bodies,
but will never change our hearts.
My sisters are still so dear to me,
closer than any kin,
and I love to recall our childhood days
and our togetherness way back then.

LET GOD

When times of trouble overwhelm you
and your feet sink in Life's sand,
step up, step up and reach for Jesus.
Hold tight to His unchanging hand.

If you're lonely and forlorn,
kneel and say a humble prayer.
Jesus is right there beside you.
His holy angels stand by you there.

He guards you every minute each day.
He share's your burdens and bears your load.
You never need to feel alone.
Jesus walks beside you on Life's road.

Let the prompting of the Holy Spirit
guard and guide you through the day.
Let God's love empower and lift you
and the Word of God light your way.

+ + +

For Heidi, Chris, Tori and Nick.

"...and, lo, I am with you alway, *even* unto the end
of the world." **Amen.**
Matthew 28:20b KJV

WILLING EAR

If you need someone to listen,
if you need a willing ear,
turn to Me. I'll be your sound post.
Remember, I am always here.

I'll not turn from you in anger
or rebuke your words unkind.
I'll just comfort, guide, console you
and in love give peace of mind.

I'm not God. I may not change things,
but I'll guide you with His love.
Just look up and ask sincerely
and I'll listen from above.

God, our Father, wants you happy,
and to live in love and health.
He wants you to care for your neighbor
as you care for and love yourself.

As the end draws ever nearer,
times will so much harder be.
But I will listen to your problems.
You can always count on Me.

I was there before creation,
being the first of Jehovah's Sons.
And I was there to bear men's burdens,
and died to guide the faithful ones.

There is nothing that can happen
that I am not sorely aware.
I can relate to all men's problems.
Remember, I was once right there.

There may be times in the darkness
when unhappy tears may flow.
But if you listen to My whispers,
then you will feel love for you glow.

TOIL

The soil may be rocky
and my rows ain't straight.
I use an old wooden board
for the garden gate.
The weeds take over
by the end of the year,
but we eat winter vegetables
without any fear.

I work in the garden
'til my muscles are sore.
I till and I hoe
'til I can't any more.
But when the day's over
I sleep like a lamb,
'cause I'm doing every day
the best that I can.

The sweat on my body
is salty but it's sweet,
and I ache in the evenings
from my head to my feet.
But I have satisfaction
when each day is through,
just knowing God is blessing
everything that I do.

So sit in your recliners
and drink beer in the heat.
Scoff at my labor
while you prop up your feet.
But I don't eat pesticides
the way that you do.
And I'll bet I'll live longer,
'cause I'm healthier than you.

I'll work in my garden
'til I'm old and I'm grey
and I'll praise Jehovah God
at the end of each day.
For He's seen fit to bless me
'cause I'm worthy in His eyes,
and I turn my hand to working
and I don't criticize.

If you turned off the boob-tube
and worked in the soil,
you'd soon have satisfaction
in a little bit of toil.
You wouldn't have the time
to sit back and criticize
and maybe what you'd learn
would make you healthy and wise.

PURPOSE

He didn't come with jewels and crown
nor gold and sweet perfume.
He didn't come with platitudes
or shouting death and doom.
He didn't come with angry words
for our transgressions bold.
He came as a helpless baby
for a gentle woman to hold.

He came in human innocence
to learn of life and love.
He came to bear our burdens
from His Father, God, above.
He came to share our sorrows
and bear our inner pain.
He came to show us how to love
and bring us peace again.

+ + +

"For God so loved the world that He gave
His only begotten Son, that whosoever believeth in Him
should not perish, but have everlasting life."
John 3:16 KJV

LOVE AND FAITH

We never know from day to day
just what God has in store
for us the minute we wake up
or walk out our front door.
So we must trust His sacred Word
and seek His guidance great.
Never trust to mortal man
nor believe in luck or fate.
Our strength will come
through love and faith
and prayer that shouldn't cease.
It's only then that happiness reigns
and hearts will rest in peace.

+ + +

"...I am come that they might have life,
and that they might have *it* more abundantly."
John 10:10b KJV

BUS EVALUATION

She came to evaluate me today
for my years of driving skill.
My stomach was doing flip-flops
and I thought I would be ill.

I quickly did the pre-trip
both outside and in the bus,
hoping I'd not forget anything
that would give her cause to fuss.

My hands were cold and clammy
and my knees began to shake.
My feet were doing a tap-dance
as I fumbled for the brake.

I put my bus into gear
and pulled out into the street
with years of driving experience to burn
and two clumsy big left feet!

I forgot to use my signals and
that stop sign flew right past.
I went to put the brake on
and my big foot hit the gas.

The bus lurched quickly forward
as the red light loomed ahead.
That poor evaluator probably
thought she'd wind up dead!

I brought that big bus to a stop
with both feet on the brake.
I knew from the look upon her face
that it was more than she could take.

She scribbled something on her pad
while her hands were shaking so...
I knew I'd failed the test right then
but she nervously told me to go.

The kids all screamed in sheer delight,
the noise nearly split my ears.
I could see the evaluator would
soon be reduced to tears.

Her eyes were as big as saucers
as she held tightly to the seat,
for I was very determined
not to go down in defeat.

I let the last child off the bus
and as my foot pressed on the gas,
I looked at my evaluator
and wondered if I would pass.

She never said a word to me
as we drove to the next school,
but her face told me as plain as day
that she thought I was a mad fool.

She was sure to pull my license now
and would probably take my keys.
She'd likely kick me off the bus
and slap my shaking knees.

But she just smiled sympathetically
when I asked her if I'd passed.
She handed me the evaluation and said,
"See you in the next driving class."

+ + +

For Kathy, Trish and Dianne in the
Harford County Transportation Department.

TEACH THE CHILDREN

Children are like sponges,
always thirsting for knowledge,
from the cradle to the grave,
from kindergarten through college.
And then beyond those years,
if instructed by the wise,
they learn the *real* purpose of life
and the difference of truth and lies.

Then if wisdom settles in
atop the knowledge they've acquired,
any future that they long for,
if they seek it they'll be hired.
If they have goals to attain
and work they do not mind,
but put their shoulders to the plow,
then certain success they'll find.

Children are the future.
They will someday take the lead.
Hopefully they'll court knowledge
and to wisdom they'll give heed.
But only if we teach them
with strength and with love,
and with knowledge of the Father
and His Son up above.

For children are *gifts* from God,
a promise of certainty
that this world will last forever,
for God made it for you and me.
So embrace His *gifts* with purpose
and hold those innocent hands
and prove to God you love Him
by heeding His commands.

Teach those little children
with love and integrity,
then you will inherit the Paradise
created for you and me.

WHAT LOVE IS

A young man once told me
that love didn't exist.
His hardness of feeling
caused my eyes to mist.
So I told him, *that* word,
though small in size
was like gold to the poor
and knowledge to the wise.
I told him in words
so simple, but true,
all that love was,
and wonderful, too.
That love was for giving,
not always to take,
and not to forget
my words for his sake.
Love doesn't hold grudges
or vengeful things do.
Love doesn't expect
the impossible from you.

Love doesn't hide sorrows
but willingly shares
the burdens and heartaches,
for love really cares.
Love doesn't blame others
for lack of its own.
Love first gives respect
before any is shown.
For such a small word
it encompasses all things,
for love from Jehovah
caused angels to sing.
Love is forgiving,
remembering we're weak.
Love makes us humble,
forgiveness to seek.
Love is a gift
first given from above.
But to make it your own
you must first *learn to love.*

THE PEACOCK

He thought himself a peacock
with his long flowing hair
as he strutted past the windows
and viewed his reflection there.

He smiled and winked and flirted
and tossed his hair aside.
He'd never wear a hat under which
that glorious hair could hide.

He smartly raised an eyebrow
as a female passed on by,
giving him a knowing look
with a hint of envy in her eye.

He walked in by the red-striped pole
as a breeze whipped through his hair.
His smile was cool and jaunty
as he sat in the barber's chair.

The peacock lost his plumage
as his tresses began to fall.
In went a vain, pompous boy...
out came a man so tall.

FEARS IN THE NIGHT

I place my hand in Yours, dear Lord,
and ask that You hold it tight,
and chase away my fears, Lord,
that plague me in the night.

This gripe of fear is painful.
It squeezes my heart so tight,
and I can scarcely breathe, Lord.
The darkness holds so much fright.

Alas, my heart does sorrow
for the things I've left undone,
but You will not let it remain so,
for the victory I know I have won.

Give me strength one more day, Lord.
Let me do what I must do,
so I can sleep with Your praise on my lips,
and dedicate my life to You.

THE LIGHTHOUSE

I walked upon the seashore
one dark and dismal day.
My heart was filled with darkness,
so much I could not pray.

I looked into the distance
and saw a brilliant light
that put the day to shame
just as if it were the night.

The beacon turned in searching
for the stranded out at sea.
I felt its radiance reaching
as it fleetingly touched me.

Jehovah is the lighthouse
and Jesus is the light
searching for the lost ones
to come in from the night.

The beacons shaft of brightness
is the love of God's Own Son,
searching for the sinners,
to save even one.

The beacon beckons daily
as Jesus softly calls,
"Come into our lighthouse.
We welcome one and all."

+ + +

Written at the request of Pastor Windell Pell
for his "Lighthouse Church of God."

RUNNING LATE

Running late! Tick, Tock!
There goes the hall clock.
Get your coat, get your hat.
Don't forget to feed the cat.

Grab your keys. Grab your purse.
Bang your elbow. Stifle a curse.
Check the stove on the way to the door.
Don't leave it on as you did before.

Hurry, hurry. Start your car.
You know you have to drive so far.
Don't run the light. Be sure to stop.
Keep alert for a roving cop.

Check your watch. Increase your speed.
Pass the traffic if you feel the need.
A little faster. Got to earn your pay.
Hey! Wait a minute...*it's Saturday!*

+ + +

For all hard-working women.

SEEK KNOWLEDGE AND WISDOM

I used to be so foolish...
I was just an upstart kid.
There really was no accounting
for the foolish things I did.
And although I was not stupid,
my actions were not good.
I did not always do
the things I knew I should.

I used not any wisdom
and my knowledge was almost nil.
All I had was stubbornness
and an ironclad will.
The thing that kept me walking
down the straight and narrow way
was the faith I had in Jesus
and the things He had to say.

He instilled in me a wonder
and a longing for a life
that was filled with Godly love
instead of grief and strife.
I have read the Bible over
and studied God's own Word
for it has life-giving meaning,
more than anything I've heard.

I've accepted Jesus' sacrifice
and God's great Gift of love,
and I know Jehovah's smiling
from His white throne up above.
He tells us to gain knowledge
and from wisdom to partake.
His TRUTH is our protection
and His Laws are for our sake.

I have yearned for Godly Wisdom
and a life lived in His care.
Ever since I can remember
God's love has been right there.
There's a fine line I am walking
but alone I'll never be.
I have a loving Companion
for Jesus walks along with me.

+ + +

"The heart of the prudent getteth knowledge;
and the ear of the wise seeketh knowledge."
Proverbs 18:15 KJV

THE SENTINEL

He stood there in the darkness
silhouetted by the moon,
unaware of the daybreak
that would be happening soon.
His ears were alert to something,
though the night was starkly still
beneath the skeletal trees
on top of the craggy hill.

His muscles were poised and ready
if a predator should appear
from the shadows of the moonlight,
evoking an unknown fear.
He'd be ready for quick action
should he be threatened by a foe.
He trembled in anticipation
for his fear he must not show.

The night became quick silver,
ever changing in the sky.
The stars dimmed in the heavens
as the darkness crept slowly by.
The cover of night lifted
with the coming of the dawn.
The sentinels watch had ended
as the darkness marched along.

One last hurrah he sounded
as if to greet the day.
He pointed his nose to heaven,
howled briefly, then slipped away.
Somewhere he'd find a respite,
a haven to rest and sleep.
But when darkness covered the mountain,
his sentinel's vigil he'd keep.

HAPPY HEART

I have so much to be thankful for;
I have a happy heart.
And of this world of sinfulness
I do not want a part.
God has blessed me richly
with joy and cheerfulness.
I'd like to share it with the world.
I have so much happiness.

When days are dark and gloomy,
I still find cause to smile.
I know that there's still sunshine
beyond those clouds all the while.
In my heart there's still gladness
that the gloom can't steal away.
I have so much joy inside me
and it lifts my heart each day.

The thing that I would tell the world
is what has been said before,
that a cheerful outlook heals the heart
of the lowly and the poor.
For worry robs one of the joy
of life and happiness
and blinds one to the *Eternal Giver*
of love and blessedness.

A happy heart stays healthy
for merriment does it good.
A smile breaks out all over
exactly as it should.
So heed these words of wisdom
for there's no better place to start
than to rid yourself of doom and gloom
and replace them with a *happy heart!*

+ + +

"A merry heart maketh a cheerful countenance:
but by sorrow of the heart the spirit is broken."
Proverbs 15:13 KJV

JUNE

The honeysuckle's blooming,
perfuming the morning air,
and nature's showing off,
dressing out everywhere.

The days are filled with sunshine
that seems to end too soon.
And hearts are filled with jubilance
to sing, "It's June! It's June!"

THE GOODNESS OF GOD

The goodness of God is everywhere.
Just open your eyes and see.
His love for us shines forth to all.
He's not partial to you or to me.
He makes the earth to shout His love
as the seasons come and they go.
How can you say that God is dead?
How can your heart not know?
He makes the sun and moon to shine.
He hangs the stars at night.
He makes our hearts to yearn for Him,
to fear His strength and might.
Oh, for the peace God freely gives
to ease our yearning hearts.
Faith and trust in His true love
is what His Truth imparts.

+ + +

"And God made two great lights; the greater light to rule the day,
and the lesser light to rule the night: *he made* the stars also."
Genesis 1:16 KJV

TRUST GOD

Sometimes people lose their way
in this old sinful land.
Satan gloats and laughs in glee
thinking he has the upper hand.
But those who stray too far afield
still have a fighting chance
to reach out to the Lord of Hope
and not give a backward glance.

Just trust the Lord with all your heart
and don't give way to sin.
Cleanse your heart of worldly *trash*
and invite your Savior in.
The understanding you may have
may not His meaning be.
He'll clear the path that you must walk
and open your eyes to see.

Fret not upon your past mistakes
for stumbling blocks are they.
Forgive yourself, as God has done
and He will light your way.
He'll guide you through life's troubling maze,
through hurtfulness and sorrow,
if you'll just turn to Him in love.
He'll guide you to a *new tomorrow.*

BEHIND THE WALL

I could hear them laughing loudly in the darkness.
They were whispering and making noises in the bed.
The squeaking of the springs made me wonder
and I imagined crazy things in my head.

There was knocking on the wall and lots of giggling.
There were groans and moans and squeals of delight.
I thought that I'd go crazy as I listened
to the noises behind the wall in the night.

I thought they might be finished in a moment,
but their energy was boundless, so it seemed.
For I could hear their playfulness at midnight
and I wondered if this was something that I dreamed.

Finally I couldn't take it any longer.
I had to see myself just what transpired.
I had to know the reason for the noises,
and what could keep them going on and fired.

I tiptoed to their door, peeked through the keyhole,
but it was dark inside. I could not see.
Suddenly I heard a yawning sigh of tiredness
that brought a sigh and relief then to me.

I crept back to bed with shoulders sagging,
imagining pouting lips and bouncing curls.
I must get some needed rest for tomorrow
my day would begin at dawn with my twin girls.

BELIEVE

Anything can happen,
if one would just believe.
Keep a positive outlook
if one deigns to receive.

Let doubts not even enter in
to cloud a trusting mind.
Just say a prayer of faithfulness.
Results will soon follow behind.

Let no one utter "maybe"
for that leaves some room for doubt.
Look up and say "I believe!"
to shut the doubters out.

Trust the strength of a Higher Power
though you may not yet see,
for God can do impossible things
with the words, "Just let it be."

So look into the mirror
and envision Jehovah there,
standing right beside you
though no one is aware.

Boost up your faith with "Yes, I can!"
and God will be your strength.
He'll guide you through the toughest times
and be there for the length.

He said He'd not forsake you.
Trust in His sacred Word.
And then the phrase, "I believe"
will be the sweetest you've ever heard.

+ + +

"And all things, whatsoever ye shall ask
in prayer, believing, ye shall receive."
Matthew 21:22 KJV

For Aunt Donna and Frances.

THE KEEPER

Be the Keeper of my heart.
Be the Watcher of my soul.
Be the Balm that sooths my fears
and warms my spirit
when hearts are cold.

Oh, Jehovah,
be my Teacher
when my heart begins to soar,
and when sorrow plucks my heartstrings,
comfort, guard me
all the more.

+ + +

For my cousin, Linda Sue.

TRACKING

I looked outside this morning
and saw a beautiful sight.
The ground was covered in pristine fluff.
It had snowed throughout the night.

The heart within me fluttered
for I saw the signs so well,
that many four-footed creatures
had visited in the dell.

My heart then took to racing
and excitement stirred within
for now I'd do some tracking
to see where these creatures had been.

I traced the tracks of foxes
that frolicked in the snow.
My curiosity peeked
and I wondered where they'd go.

The deer stayed near the tree line,
their tracks running parallel.
There was a doe and two small yearlings,
as close as I could tell.

The rabbit tracks ran rampant,
crisscrossing everywhere.
No doubt a predator was close by
and gave them quite a scare.

The paw prints of a frisky squirrel
would start beneath a tree,
then go off through the woodland
where no one else could see.

The raccoon's paws shown plainly
in the snow beside the creek.
I hoped to creep up on them
and quietly take a peek.

But the bandits were illusive
and their tracks led far away.
Perhaps I'd come upon them
but it wouldn't be today.

I walked on through the woodland
and saw tracks both large and small,
made by many four-footed friends
but the strangest of them all

were the tracks of two huge feet
with five toes big and bare.
I could not help but believe
that Sasquatch had walked in there.

I walked back to my cabin
with the tracks running in my mind.
Yet, the strangest tracks of all
were the ones I left behind.

THERE IS A TIME

A flower blooms and then it fades
and dies in winters cold.
A child is born, becomes a man
and he, then too, grows old.

There is a time for everything
that God created on earth,
from plants and animals, birds and fish,
and babies sweet at birth.

There is a time for learning,
of wisdom and knowledge, too.
There is a time when learning's done
and then you have to *do*.

There is a time for everything
beneath the heavens above.
But time would be worth nothing
if it didn't begin with God's love.

+ + +

"To every *thing there is* a season, and a time
to every purpose under the heaven:..."
Ecclesiastes 3:1 KJV

BRIGHT STAR

She is my sister's mother
and was my daddy's wife.
She's the woman I admire,
for she gave me life.
She's the friend that I cherish,
the voice that I hear,
the comfort that I feel
when she's standing near.
She's the guidance and the wisdom
of ages long since past.
She's the love of the motherhood
over centuries amassed.
She's the bright star of the morning,
the glow in my day.
She's the smile in my spirit
that I give away.
She's what songs are sung for,
she's the brightness above.
She was my daddy's wife,
but, she's the mother that I love.

+ + +

For my mother, my bright star.

I SEE HIM

I see Him in the heavens
when the stars shine so bright.
And beyond the farthermost moonbeam
I search for Him at night.

I see Him in the sunshine
that kisses the flowers face.
I see Him and I feel Him
for He is in *every place.*

+ + +

"And he that seeth me seeth him that sent me."
John 12:45 KJV

MOMENTS IN PRAYER

These moments in prayer I spend with You,
these moments I spend in thought,
lead me to know how inadequate I am,
so neglectful to do what I ought.

My guilt comes to fore and my shame overwhelms,
but, still my struggles arise,
to reach out to You, my Redeemer, my God,
and You wipe the tears from my eyes.

How blest I do feel to call on Your Name,
to know You are always there.
Without a doubt I know You as "Friend",
yes, I know that You'll always care.

These moments I spend should be hours and days,
a lifetime of worship to You.
For I feel Your Presence, Your love hold me fast.
Keep me near You, whatever I do.

Should I be tempted to stray from the path
of righteousness You set before,
correct me, I pray, and point me again
to the light from Your open door.

+ + +

"Hear, O Jehovah, when I call with my voice,
And show me favor and answer me. Concerning you
my heart has said: "Seek to find my face, YOU people."
Your face, O Jehovah, I shall seek to find. Do not
conceal your face from me. Do not in anger turn your
servant away. My assistance you must become. Do not
forsake me and do not leave me, O my God of salvation."
Psalms 27:7-9 NWT

CORN SHOCK MEMORIES

Harvest time is nigh once more
and I can see so clear,
sweet memories of long ago
of a time I hold so dear...
of corn stalks standing in a field
tied up in shocks like gold,
and every one a playground
for children adventurous and bold.

I can see my siblings
playing 'hide and seek' in there,
pretending they were conquering kings
in a far-off land somewhere,
hiding inside the corn shocks
and spying on their foe,
savoring the momentary shade,
letting imaginations grow.

I was an Indian princess,
and Wayne was a gallant knight,
while Elmer played a soldier
ready for the fight.
Delain and little Windell
were cowboys through it all,
and we played in those dry corn shocks
till the night began to fall.

Sisters Gene and Barbara
played in the corn shocks too,
along with little Dallas
and a stray cat or two.
No doubt mousing was their objective,
but fun was our main quest,
and hiding inside the corn shocks
was playtime at its best.

Now when I see golden cornfields
being cut by big machines,
there are no golden corn shocks
to spark young children's dreams.
So I'll share these special memories
with those I hold so dear,
and reminisce of happy times
while we're blessed to still be here.

+ + +

Written for Uncle Wayne at his request for
sweet memories of youth.

MY PRAYER FOR YOU

Today I said a prayer for you
for you've been sad so long,
that God would straighten out the curves
when things seem to go wrong.

I know He heard the words I said.
I prayed so hard, you know.
I asked that He would light your path
and show you where to go.

Sometimes our battles seem so hard
where loved ones are concerned,
and letting go of heartaches
is the hardest lessons learned.

But if we let God take the lead
and guide us through life's maze,
He'll show us blessings yet untold
to brighten all our days.

I asked God's love to strengthen you.
Like me, you're sometimes weak.
He told us we would find Him here
if we diligently would seek.

Just look beyond the cares and woes
that plague your heart each day,
and you will find His comforting love
if you earnestly to Him pray.

+ + +

"And ye shall seek me, and find *me,* when ye
shall search for me with all your heart.
And I will be found of you, saith the LORD:..."
Jeremiah 29:13, 14a KJV

THINGS OF THE PAST

The old ways are the best ways.
That's what old folks recall.
The memories we have of the past
are always the best of all.
And if, perchance, we should share
some memories that intertwine,
they become exclusively "ours",
and not just yours or mine.

Sometimes it's nice to sit awhile
to dream and reminisce
of friends you knew so long ago,
a smile, a first sweet kiss.
And if a word or gesture
should spark a memory dear,
it's strange that you forget a name
but recall a face so clear.

Sometimes a rhyme or limerick
causes pictures to freely flow
into your activated mind
sending thoughts to and fro.
When you decide to spend some time
with memories of the past,
time seems to pass so quickly by,
but the warmth of memories last.

The brain is a true phenomenon
with capacity to endlessly store
all the happenings of today
and all that came before.
It's all a sweet reminder
of the Creator's love that lasts,
to link us still through His will
in memories of things of the past.

THE POWER OF GOD

Don't deny the power of God
by saying He does not heal,
that today He does not work that way
when His powers are truly real.

Don't say He doesn't speak to us,
no voices we should hear.
He communicates more often than you know
for His angels are always near.

Just pray with a heart full of love.
Believe what His Word speaks.
Be lowly of heart, not haughty or proud.
God hears the prayers of the meek.

God hears the prayers of the humble of heart.
He hears and answers the cries.
And for those who say He doesn't heal us today,
God's power they foolishly deny.

You tie His hands with words of doubt.
In your ignorance, you won't let Him in
to use His power to help you out
of the problems that led you to sin.

I tell you a Truth, prayer changes things
if you don't let Satan deceive.
The clouds of doubt will roll right out
when first you begin to believe.

So take His Word for what it is...
God's power of Truth and Love.
Throw upon Him your troubles and sorrow,
for God truly reigns from above.

+ + +

"And all things, whatsoever ye shall ask in
prayer, believing, ye shall receive."
Matthew 21:22 KJV

MY FOUR-FOOTED FRIENDS

I look toward the goat house
whenever I go out
and listen for their ringing bells
to see if they're about.

Then I remember they're not there.
I sold them some time ago.
I seem to see their big brown eyes.
Oh, how I miss them so.

They use to run and cry for joy
to see me come outside.
I hid my sorrow in the silence
when I really should have cried.

Now the tears are in my heart,
no more to see them play.
But I have many memories
of younger, brighter days.

They'd skip and run and bleat their joy
while playing in the sun.
Or just laze around on their bench
until the day was done.

Sometimes they'd press so close to me
and I'd brush their silky hair.
They seemed to love me with their eyes,
so glad to have me there.

Now silence greets me in the yard.
No more I'll see their face.
I'll not forget, though years may pass,
for none will take their place.

+ + +

For my beautiful *Ryan's Beauty* and her
son, *Ryan's Jet Magnum and Maggie.* I'll always love you all.

Jesus saith unto them, *"I am the way, the truth, and the life: no man cometh unto the Father, but by me."*
John 14:6 KJV

FAMILY LOVE... THE WAY

God created the family unit
in the union of Adam and Eve,
but He doesn't sanction gossip
or the proverbial pet peeve.
Those are Satan's little playthings,
for dissension is his forte'.
He delights in family squabbles
when his game they choose to play.

God tells us of the pitfalls,
of the snares and Satan's lies,
and His Word that goes unheeded
corrupts the family ties.
If we allow the stones
of hatred to creep in,
they will destroy family love
and let old Satan win.

Dissension does not fill our pockets
nor put food upon our dish.
It does not make us happy
nor fulfill a secret wish.
But it does create a problem
that destroys a family trust.
Forgiveness is a virtue;
to cultivate it is a *must...*

If one is to be a *Christian*
and live a life of peace,
then playing Satan's games
is a practice that must cease.
We cannot choose our family
for that choice is made above.
And He makes the perfect choice
and tenders it with love.

We must take His Grand Example
and *honor* parents too,
for He trusted us to them
and before *His Plan* is through,
we will all respect each other,
learning how, with love, to give.
Then we will have come full circle
and have learned the *WAY* to live.

+ + +

Honour thy father and thy mother:
that thy days may be long upon the land
which the LORD thy God giveth thee.
Exodus 20:12 KJV

LOVE LIGHT

I saw upon your face today
the brightness of your smile.
I knew you'd tell me of the reason
if I waited for a while.
And sure enough, your words came tumbling
in such a joyous roll,
and I could see that love came calling,
and that it touched your soul.

Your eyes lit up, your voice just sang,
your words danced in the air.
Your heart was full to overflowing,
of love you had to share.
I could not help but smile a bit
as you bubbled a minute or two,
and I thought as I listened to your joy,
"love sure looks good on you."

I wish you all of life's greatest joys
and the blessings of God above.
I wish you health and a measure of wealth,
but mostly, I wish you love.
And of life's treasures, I wish you success
in all you choose to do.
And I can tell, you'll do very well,
for "love sure looks good on you!"

+ + +

For Joanne, with God's blessings.

SENSELESS WAR

Oh, Lord, I feel such sorrow
for the imminence of war...
a sorrow of such magnitude
I've never felt before.

There's a chance I'll lose a loved one,
and *they'll* lose so many too.
War just has no conscience.
We'll *all* lose when it's through.

Is it really patriotic
to take a life away
or is the motive really "greed",
the trademark of today?

The leaders of our countries
argue, push and shove
in fulfillment of the scriptures
handed down from God above.

There may soon be many widows
and orphans in our land,
and the hearts of countless parents
will grieve throughout the land.

Oh, Lord, please intervene
so Your world will not be lost
and the lives of Your children
will not have to pay the cost

for all the greedy barons
whose greed will only grow
because the love of God
they just don't want to know.

SILENT ANGELS

There are many silent angels
who walk this earth today,
who hear the cries of distress
and touch us when we pray.

We can see them in a friendly smile
or in someone's twinkling eyes.
We know they lend a helping hand
as we hush a baby's cries.

And when our hearts are full of gloom,
they help us see the Light
of Life that God meant us to have
to help us through the dark night.

When we feel alone without a friend,
they'll give us comfort too,
and guide us toward the strength within
that God gives to me and you.

Our angels will never leave our side.
They're just a prayer away.
God sent them as our Spiritual Companions
to help us every day.

So be glad for the silent angels
who originate from God above,
for God always gives the best of gifts,
because He sends them with His love.

NEVER GO HOME

The house was smaller than I remembered.
The neighbors were old or no longer there.
The friends I knew I'd long since forgotten.
The ones I'd loved now no longer cared.

The yard was rutted and full of weeds.
My favorite tree had long been cut down.
The hill I played on as a young girl
was now a freeway that led into town.

The stream I played in was filled with stones.
The water dried up or had gone another way.
The tree house I played in had rotted with time,
leaving fond memories to smile at today.

One lesson I've learned from this visitation,
is things are never the same as then.
Memories are better than stark actualities,
for truly, you can never go home again.

REMEMBER?

Do you remember me?
I'm the little girl
who sat upon your knee.
You combed my golden hair
and called me "honeybee".
Papa, do you remember me?

I looked into his faded eyes
behind the vacant stare
and tried to find the loving man
I knew had once lived there.
There was no recognition,
no warmth, no, not a word.
There was no inclination
that he had even heard.

I put my arms around him,
his shoulders gaunt and thin,
and prayed to God in heaven
that he would let me in.
But hope was quickly fading
and I held him close in fear.
Then behind his faded eyes
slipped a single salty tear.

Do you remember me?
Papa, I'm the little girl
who sat upon your knee.
You combed my golden hair
and called me your "honeybee".
Papa, do you remember me?

SUPERSTITION

I don't believe in witches
with their warts and boney noses,
nor ghosts and goblins flying through the night.
I don't believe in bats that change
to vampires seeking blood,
then flit across the moon's eerie light.

I don't think ebony felines
cause misfortune to us befall,
no more than wrapping wood keeps it at bay.
Spilled salt thrown over the shoulder
is just grit upon the floor
to be vacuumed at the close of the day.

I'm brave in horror movies
when my friends all cringe and cry.
I laugh at boys who give the girls a scare.
I've never been a sissy when
I've seen a gory sight,
and haven't felt standing end neck hair.

I don't think of poltergeists when
things fall as I walk by.
I'm not afraid to stroll the park at night.
But, please, as you say goodbye,
would you leave the door ajar,
and snap on that little angel night light?

PUT YOUR HANDS TOGETHER

Put your hands together and love Him.
Close your eyes and whisper His sweet Name.
Bow your head and worship there before Him.
Thank the Lord He loved you when He came.

Put your hands together and adore Him.
Spread them wide and welcome Him come in.
Tell Him that you love Him most sincerely.
You know that He's forgiven all your sin.

You know He only wants you to be happy.
He showers you with blessings from above.
His love for you is greater than forever,
so, put your hands together in His love.

THE FARMER

What if all the grocery stores
would suddenly become bare,
and you went to do your shopping
and there were no groceries there?

And, what if all the restaurants
had to close their doors
because there was no food to cook
and none to buy from stores?

Just think! The lowly farmers
would become our V.I.P.'s.
They'd be the latest millionaires
and charge just what they please.

Our farmers feed the nations
with no thanks or gratitude.
And often when they're spoken of,
the comments can be rude.

They bend their backs long hours
to plow and plant the earth.
They claim God as their Partner,
helping nature give new birth.

They sweat and pray and worry
that the weather will be kind.
They thank God for His mercy
when He eases troubled mind.

Then through long summer hours
they hoe and harvest too.
They can, preserve and transport
their produce on to you.

So when you do your shopping,
remember the toil the farmers bear
because with God as their Partner,
they feed the world with care.

RAIN IN DISGUISE

It is quicksilver
on glass.
It is a path left
by hot tears.
It is Nature's spittle
sliding earthward.
It is a snail's
vapor trail.
It is a microbe's view
of a mighty rushing river.
It is all these things
in the guise
of raindrops
on my window pane.

GOD LIVES

God lives in the Ghettoes. I saw Him there today.
He was in the face of a little child
who sat alone to play.

God lives down in Harlem.
He fills dark hearts with joy.
I heard Him in the mournful song
of a little Negro boy.

God lives in the sandy desert
among the shifting hills.
He comforts hearts of Bedouin children
and heals their many ills.

God lives in the lofty mountains.
He lives in the meadows too.
You can search for God all over the earth,
but He lives right there in you.

He lives right there in you.
He lives right there in you.

OLD?

Forty isn't old, Mom.
You've hardly any grey hair.
The children are barely grown and
you've a lot of spunk in there.

Fifty isn't old, Mom.
It's half a century, it's true.
But there's still a half to go yet and
plenty of things to do.

Sixty isn't old, Mom.
You've got grandbabies on your lap.
They keep you young and running and
there's some zing left in your snap.

Seventy isn't old, Mom.
Why, Dad's still pinching the girls.
You've got the brightest of smiles, Mom,
and there's gold in some of your curls.

Eighty isn't old, Mom.
So you use a cane to walk.
Your sight may be a little dimmer,
but you *never* miss a word of talk.

Ninety isn't *really* old, Mom........
YES *it is!*

SOMEBODY CARES

Somebody cares about you.
Somebody knows your pain.
Somebody prays to God above when
tears fall like the rain.

Somebody holds you closer when
storm clouds gather 'round.
Somebody whispers your name to God when
your heart makes not a sound.

Somebody loves you dearly and
all of your sorrows share.
Somebody's with you each moment, for
Somebody really cares.

+ + +

"...as I was with Moses, so I will be with thee:
I will not fail thee, nor forsake thee."
Joshua 1:5b KJV

IS THIS REALLY CHRISTMAS?

The air is peaceful, cold and still.
The stars twinkle at night.
The cat slinks in the shadows while
birds twitter in the moonlight.
But...is this *really* Christmas?

Shoppers scurry downtown,
purchases piling high.
Nervous voices chatter,
weary as the hours fly by.
But...is *this* really Christmas?

Footsteps tread through the snow,
a deliberate, peaceful walk,
into church to kneel and worship.
There is no need to talk.
This...is really Christmas!

OCTOBER'S MAN

My son, you are a man, you say, with
all life's childishness washed away.
You stand so tall for the world to see.
You tower a foot well over me.

Switch I, no more, your hinder part when
thoughtless actions break my heart.
But I stand by and for you pray that
you will be a man some day.

A man you claim you are right now.
My wish is to believe in you somehow.
And while I give your years the nod,
a *MAN* is *unashamed* to love God.

+ + +

"Train up a boy according to the way for him;
even when he grows old he will not turn aside
from it."
Proverbs 22:6 NWT

SILENT HUNTER

He climbs upon a silver thread
and shimmies up and down
with a quickness that belies his
leggyness.
One would expect great clumsiness
with limbs the girth of his body, yet
agility is his niche
in Life.
He sits upon his web in watchfulness,
awaiting unsuspecting prey.
Busily, he spins his pretty
silver web.
Watching, watching,
he spins the day away.
Silently, he suns himself
upon his jeweled throne,
content to sit as the sun
climbs high,
steadily advancing on entangled
winged prey.
He dines alone,
savoring the struggling fly.

+ + +

"...and the hypocrite's hope shall perish:
Whose hope shall be cut off, and whose
trust *shall be* a spider's web."
Job 8:13b, 14 KJV

MOTHER, PRAY WITH ME

A little girl lay sleeping,
her head on mother's knee.
She whispered in her slumber,
"Mother, pray with me."

Mother stopped her reading,
her mind raced back in years
to a little girl that knelt
in the torment of her tears.

She had begged her mother when
she was just past three,
"Mommy, tell me stories, and
Mommy, pray with me."

The little girl was carried and
tucked into her bed.
Mother knelt there praying and
kissed her daughters head.

Mother would remember, no matter
time and tide shall be, when
her sleeping child had whispered,
"Mother, pray with me."

+ + +

"And these words, which I command thee this
day, shall be in thine heart:
And thou shalt teach them diligently unto thy
children, and shalt talk of them when thou sittest
in thine house, and when thou walkest by the way,
and when thou liest down, and when thou risest up."
Deuteronomy 6:6, 7 KJV

YESTERDAY'S DREAMS

I looked into my yesterdays and
found you smiling there.
I washed your face and kissed your cheek.
I combed your curly hair.

And when you fell and skinned your knee,
I hugged you in my arms.
I dried your tears and held you close.
I kept you from life's harms.

I took you to the church each week and
taught you how to pray.
I asked God's help to guide you straight and
keep you from sin's way.

Now that my tomorrows have
become my yesterday's dreams,
my little boy has become a man...
and forgotten me, it seems.

+ + +

For Alen, my yesterday's child.

I AM LIFE

I was there at the Creation and watched as
He gave them part of me.
And for all eternity I was wounded and
bled with their sin.
From deep within the earth I cried out as
part of me ebbed away.
I was slighted beneath the feet of men,
wounded, nevermore to win.

I was exalted when Solomon prayed for
the wisdom to rule, then
forgotten as the Chosen Land was
divided and conquered anew.
I was reborn as the star shown on the
Chosen One's holy face.
I heard His cry asking for forgiveness for
all and was pierced through.

Elated, I found new freedom in the spirit of
a far virgin land.
I struggled in the growing pains of
the wretched, lost and poor.
I was held up in the name of Freedom for
oppressed mankind.
I was used, abused, and choked,
struggling to open the door.

I writhed in anguish while millions
died in the cold prison camps.
I lay, spread out on battlefields of
years, wasted and worn;
hallowed once more each year on the
anniversary of His earthly birth.
How heavy the burdens and sorrows that
I have long borne.

I am *LIFE.* Will I yet endure?

PEACEFUL HIDEAWAY

I wish I had a hideaway place to
go and spend some time.
A place to pray and purge my soul of
the secret sinful crime.
The crime of anger, lust or sloth,
the crime of discontent.
A place to simmer in peaceful thoughts for
which my soul was meant.

If I could find a hideaway place where
fragrance fills the air,
I'd wash myself in quiet dreams and
rest my heart in care.
I'd sit and ponder on troubled things.
I would try to find a way to
solve each problem that looms so large
but only for that one day.

If I could find that hideaway place,
I'd search for the tides of love.
I'd float on currents of peaceful thoughts and
lift my soul above.
I'd find a way to live with man,
to show him what I see.
I'd pray to God for understanding,
to let it begin with me.

+ + +

"...he went up into a mountain apart to pray: and
when the evening was come, he was there alone."
Matthew 14:23b KJV

THE TOUCH OF GOD

Here I am, standing on nothing,
staring around at empty space.
A blanket of darkness coldly enfolds me.
An empty void caresses my face.

A brilliance never seen before
passes by me close at hand.
Then I remember happier times
in a green, lush, beautiful land.

There's a silver silence all about me,
so heavy that it presses down.
I hear my own heart pounding loudly,
a thumping, pulsing, drum-like sound.

And then I feel a warmth engulf me,
a Comforting Peace holds me tight.
I close my eyes and I see clearly
the face of God in the night.

I had to know this stark aloneness
and feel this empty far-out space,
to know the joy and love of God,
and feel His eyeball, face to face.

+ + +

"For now we see through a glass, darkly;
but then face to face: now I know in part;
but then shall I know even as also I am known."
I Corinthians 13:12 KJV

OVER THE HILL

At this particular time of year
when days are short and cold,
I don't dwell on time that passes
or feelings of growing old.
But I do think of those I love,
how precious a gift they are, and
I'd rather have their sweet embrace,
for it's better than gold by far.

I don't need a special occasion
to send them wishes of joy and wealth,
for every day I thank Jehovah
for giving us love and health.
For health is better than any diamonds
and love is better than gold.
And though time robs us of many things,
it is not what makes us old.

Age is a situation that
time will not erase,
and lines are a badge of courage
that you wear upon your face.
Love makes a deeper imprint
that etches across our heart
and leaves a path time can't destroy
where eternity has it's start.

Whenever the days get even shorter
and the nights turn colder still,
I think of the years that quickly pass
and I've crested another "hill".
I stand at the edge of the mythical horizon
where the sun will descend and set,
and vow to Jehovah and all mankind,
"Hey! I'm *not over the hill just yet!*"

PETITION TO GOD

Give me strength for today, Lord,
and faith in a new tomorrow,
so that I may not seek trouble
or other problems borrow.

Help me to cope, oh Lord,
when troubles tend to arise,
and look for your sweet blessings
in the bright, sunny skies.

Teach me to listen closely
for the music and song
of Nature's melodies
all the day long.

May I show appreciation
for Your loving grace,
to let Your love shine
in the smile upon my face.

Instill in me patience
when turmoil swirls near,
to lean on your mercy
and not harbor fear.

Help me to understand
when confusion and pain
batter my aching heart
and only teardrops I gain.

Give me the refuge I seek,
and peace so sublime.
Guide me, Lord, protect me,
one day at a time.

+ + +

"In God *is* my salvation and my glory:
the rock of my strength, *and* my refuge,
is in God."
Psalms 62:7 KJV

FAREWELL, MY LOVE

She looked into his eyes
at the distant vacant stare,
trying to find a semblance
of the man she knew was there.

He had been her greatest admirer,
and she his life-long friend.
She never foresaw the day when
the love they shared would end.

She squeezed his hand so gently,
then turned to wave goodbye.
She didn't see the tear that slipped
silently from his eye.

She couldn't know his awareness
was just beneath the skin
and that he suffered inwardly
for the state his mind was in.

Still, he knew they had a connection,
a love that would always be.
He'd show her that love again someday
when God set his spirit free.

+ + +

For Nancy & Ronald Reagan.

VALLEY OF DREAMS

There's a field in yonder valley
that is special just to me,
where every sort of flower grows
beneath a giant tree.

With its branches all extended
it reaches far and wide,
giving wildlife homes and refuge,
a safe haven in which to hide.

Its leaves are cool and shady
and rustle in the air,
murmuring sounds of comfort
and security for residents there.

It's a sanctum for the weary,
a respite from the world.
It's a rest within the maelstrom
where all cares are left unfurled.

Where is this sacred valley
and the caring field of dreams?
Just look beyond yon rainbow
between the stitches of mind-game seams.

HEY, DOCTOR!

I called the doctor today
because I was hurting so.
I had a sinus infection
and blood was in every blow.
I told him about my aches and pains
although I could hardly speak.
He said I sounded just fine to him
and to call again in a week.

Two days went by so quickly
and it hurt even to breathe,
so I called the doctor again
to see if he'd give me some ease.
I told him about the greenish slime
and that I thought I had an infection.
He'd have to see for himself, he said,
after he'd made an inspection.

He didn't give me an appointment,
but said he'd call back soon.
I waited with soaring fevers
then I called the next day at noon.
I told him my ears were paining me,
and my throat was red and raw.
My glands were throbbing like a ticking clock
and were the biggest I ever saw.

Again, he squelched my urgent call.
He didn't seem a bit upset.
He said in that cool condescending tone,
"I haven't lost a patient yet."
In a rasping high-pitched squeaky voice
with fever burning in my head,
I told him not to bother himself any more,
I didn't need him 'cause I just dropped dead!

WINTER'S REALITIES AND EXPECTATIONS

When it's cold and snowing
and the wind is stiffly blowing,
winter's icy fingers reach far and wide.
One's spine starts to quiver
and the flesh begins to shiver.
One snuggles beneath blankets warm to hide.

The snowflakes all are whirling,
a-twisting and a-twirling,
then settle in a coverlet of white.
Little creatures scurry.
They're all in such a hurry
to find shelter and comfort for the night.

The house is warm and cozy
and children's cheeks are rosy.
They're anxious for the morning to arise.
The fire is brightly glowing
while outside it's fiercely snowing.
Tomorrow will once more bring sunny skies.

SIMPLE TIMES

I am convinced that life was simpler
many years ago.
All the hardships that people endured,
we shall never know.
The air was cleaner, the water more pure,
the food was better still.
The eye could feast on yon horizon
and never gets its fill.
The grass seemed greener without the chemicals
that kill the weeds today.
And though people worked from sun to moon,
peaceful sleep was not far away.
Stress was not part of their day back then;
they lived the best way they could,
appreciating all the things they had,
treating others just as they should.
They filled each day with satisfying work,
and if things were not as they planned,
it wasn't for the lack of trying,
for perfection was not in demand.
They wanted a dry roof over head
and sufficient to eat and to dress.
Some lived with good and plenty
while many lived with much less.

One thing in common most people had
was a deep faith in God and love,
respect and principals of how to live,
and a friendship with the Father above.
And never a night did they close their eyes
without a thankful prayer
for home and family and love of God,
grateful He is always there.
So take me back to a simpler time
where laughter and love rule the day.
Where less is more, where true things count,
and love grows when you give it away.
Take me back to when reverence mattered,
and where fear of our Great God above
lead us to treat all men as brothers
and people knew that *God **is** love.*

I WALK ALONE

I walk a path that's hard and rocky
and I walk this path alone,
without a fleshly brother to guide me,
without a friend to call my own.

My path has many stumbling stones
that wound me every day.
The only way that I can endure
is to bow my head and pray.

There are roadblocks of every shape and size.
There are traps in many places.
So, I have to look for comfort
in the smiles on Christian faces.

This path I walk is long and narrow
and I sometimes slip and fall,
but there's always Someone close to catch me.
He hears me whenever I call.

Sometimes I cry such bitter tears
to hold a loved one's hand
and pray to God the one I love
will really understand.

But I can tell from the words spoken
and from the harsh cold tone
that I am destined in this life, at least,
to walk this path alone.

THREAD OF LIFE

I cannot give of myself
lest I give of Thee.
For You are I,
and I am You.
Separated,
I cannot live apart from Thee.
And though oft' I estrange
myself from Thee,
yet always I seek the umbilical
that ties me ever to Thy bosom.
Alone,
I am nothing.
With Thee,
I am the
Universe of Life.

THE CLOWN

He has a painted face
and a bulbous rubber nose.
He wears a stylish derby
decorated with a rose.
His hair is wild and woolly
and as orange as can be.
He's such a silly clown,
there for every "child at heart" to see.
But, oh, there's so much more to him;
deep down inside he's sad,
so he makes those funny faces
so that others hearts feel glad.
If they could hear his breaking heart
or see the tears he cries,
they'd know the reason why
he has such sad, soulful eyes.
But he hides his feelings well
behind his painted-on smile
and brings to others laughter
if just for a little while.
Then when all the crowds diminish
and only starlight fills the skies,
he washes away the paint
and reveals his pain-filled eyes.
His daylight hours are fantasy-filled,
his night time hours are real.
And no one knows that behind the paint
just how badly he really feels.
When the blanket of night fades away
and the darkness disappears,
he hides the sadness behind his mask
and once more the clown appears.

I SEARCHED FOR YOU

When I was a child I searched for You
with yearning in my heart.
But it seemed to me Your world and mine
were always far apart.

It did not make me yearn the less
as years sped by so fast,
for truth seemed to beckon the harder
as the present became the past.

Often I came so close to You
and You touched me in my heart.
You knew me when I was a stranger
and I knew we would never part.

I loved You with all of my being
though I never knew Your Name.
I was old before I met You
and my life has not been the same.

You touched me with truth and beauty,
and made me hunger for more;
for accurate knowledge I searched
and You lovingly opened the door.

Then I took the plunge of faithfulness
and You smiled and took my hand
and led me to truth and contentment
so I, at last, could understand.

Why did years have to pass like night
without knowledge of passing time,
when all I had to do was accept You
and realize You could always be mine?

Wisdom only comes with aging.
It's a fact too true to deny.
And it's only when we come to acceptance
that we learn all the reason's "why".

SURVIVOR

I survived the Holocaust,
although I wasn't there.
I came through the Depression
but I was too young to care.

I lived through the fifties
and the flower-child generation,
where smoking pot was the "thing to do"
and free love was ruination.

The sixties brought the mini skirts
and short-shorts were the rage.
And soon the morals of the world
were blasted across the news page.

The seventies bred its problems too,
with drugs of every kind.
It seems the world just could not wait
to blow it's drug-filled mind.

The eighties caused a revolution
of a very different sort,
when free love resulted in pregnancies
and mothers found clinics to abort.

Now that the nineties are almost over,
I wonder for what they'll be known?
Will it be for *all* of these former things
or something unique of their own?

There is disrespect as never before,
a love-hate situation,
that's plunged the youth to depths of despair
and ultimate degradation.

There are crimes of theft, murder and rape
on every corner, it seems,
and children are haunted with increasing fear,
even at night in their dreams.

There are storms so violent and earthquakes too,
that split the earth apart,
and put the fear of God in man
that would still a gallant heart.

But hate survives the toughest blows
and comes back stronger than before.
So as these years close in on the century,
this generation will be tested the more.

I think of all the years gone by
and the problems that I've survived,
and wonder how much longer that God will let
this evil generation stay alive?

There's a revolution of a different sort
that was predicted so long ago,
a movement toward the spiritual things
that hungry hearts want to know.

The truth of the sacred secrets of God
has given me the strength to survive
in this evil-infested world of sin.
I know that Jehovah is *still alive!*

Yes, I'm a survivor, with God to thank
in this world of turmoil and doubt.
And whether there's happiness, sorrow or pain,
I'm going to live it all out.

And when the nineties come to an end,
and this century comes to the close,
what this world will be is anyone's guess
and the future..*only God knows!*

WINGS

I put her on a pedestal
where she didn't want to be.
I placed her on a mountain top
so high she could not see.

I listened to her every word
as if it were the law
and obeyed her every little whim
because I was in awe.

And then as I grew older,
I learned she was no saint.
Reality then struck me down
so hard that I could faint.

I could see she was only human
as tears streamed down her cheeks.
And in her human frailties
I saw she could be weak.

It was then that I embraced her
and held her, oh, so tight.
I learned in just that moment
that it was I who held the might.

But I chose to be the protector
of the weak and fragile things.
She was a stricken angel
but I found she still had wings.

+

Yes, she had wings on the spirit of her heart,
although it wasn't wise to be that way.
She had wings, though she tried to deny them,
but the wings on her heart were there to stay.

I WISH YOU LOVE

I wish you love
so sweet and pure,
unmade by human hands.
A love that's kind,
considerate, true,
not one that makes demands.

I wish you joy
more precious than gold
and peace without any measure.
And last of all
I wish you hope,
more precious than any treasure.

These wishes I make
from a humble heart
that was touched by deepest love,
created by invisible
caring hands,
and given by God above.

HER PRAYERS

"I'll keep you in my prayers," she said,
her eyes filled with concern.
I could feel the Christ-like love
deep down inside me burn.
Her countenance glowed as she spoke.
Her words were as silver and gold.
She made those words sound, oh, so sweet,
like Jesus' love so bold.
I could not help the warmth I felt
as barriers dissipated.
Here, at last, was agape' love
for which my heart had waited.
She proved to be a friend indeed
when my spirit dipped so low,
always giving a willing ear
while patience and kindness she'd show.

"I'll keep you in my prayers", she said
as she warmly squeezed my hand.
It was as if Jesus was touching my heart
and I began to understand
the depth of His compassion,
the height of His sweet, pure love
that radiated like the morning sun
that shown down from above.
My heart then swelled with gratitude
for her, my partner in prayer.
I knew whenever my spirit lagged,
that she'd always be right there.
I thanked my God in heaven above
for such a friend as she,
because she loved with agape' love,
and she meant it just for me.

+ + +

For Jackie Lee, my friend.

I AM LONELY

I am lonely, Lord, though I'm not alone.
There are people around me all day.
And I have friends and family dear,
but no one to love in a special way.
I am content with my lot in life.
I have done the best I can do.
But there's no one to help me
through struggles and strife,
so, Lord, I humbly turn to You.

Help me to face my problems each day,
to stand up though my knees are weak.
I find that I have feet of clay,
so Your strength, Lord, daily I seek.
Send me the comfort of Your sweet love.
Shield me beneath Your outstretched arm.
Give me protection from up above.
Let me fear no one who'll do me harm.
Touch my soul with Your tender mercy.
Change in me this heart of stone.
Make clear my eyes that I may see
that with You, Dear Lord, I'm *never* alone.

+ + +

"...I will never leave thee, nor forsake thee."
Hebrews 13:5 KJV

FRAGILITY OF LIFE

Human life is fragile,
like a vapor in the wind.
It visits for a little while,
and then it's gone again.
Life's fragility is phenomenal
and can too soon be gone.
But that was not in God's Great Plan.
It should go on and on.
Life is like a puff of smoke
and will eventually dissipate,
never more to reassemble,
ever changing to spiritually relate.
"Life is relative", some may say,
but to what, is the inquisition.
It leads one to realize
that we're not in the best position
to bargain for a single breath
nor moment more of life,
for we cannot add another day
by coping successfully with strife.
Life must be lived by moments,
not squandered in wanton whim,
for we would not have it yet at all
if it were not for the love of Him
Who chose to suffer for our sins
and then to hang and die.
He even begged forgiveness for us
with His last breath and cry.
So, though life may be fragile,
we must live it at our best.
We'll have lived life to its fullest
when we go to our final rest.

THE WINTER STORM

Oh, the world is beautiful,
a painting all in white,
that began to create a landscape
of beauty throughout the night.
So when the morning arrived,
the scenery had all been changed.
The woodland had dressed in white,
its appearance all rearranged.
The fluffy frozen cotton
that now kissed each bush and tree,
became a canopy of beauty
for all the world to see.
The birds sit on the feeders
and dine in noisy throngs,
then reward the listening ear
with sweet melodious songs.
The morning sun has risen
but it's hidden from our sight
by the snow clouds heavy laden
with the blanket of pure white.
Now the winter fire is blazing
and the hearth is toasty warm.
And I doze beside the wood stove,
safe from the white winter storm.

MY GIFT OF LOVE

He loaned it to me for a while
and allowed me to learn and grow.
I put it in all my emotions
and the things He wanted me to know.
I gave it all of my joys and sorrows
and my secrets over the years.
I wrote down my deepest feelings
and then watered it all with my tears.
I threw out all inhibitions
and wrote what lay deep in my heart,
then read it over and over,
tore it up and made a new start.
No subject was safe from my pencil.
No topic escaped my keen hand.
But the spiritual side kept on calling
and I felt it take on a demand.
My "gift" grew better with aging,
maturing with meaning and grace.
It filled me with deep satisfaction.
I felt I had found my true place.
But a gift so intense and precious
cannot be kept just for one.
It must be shared with others
to grow in their hearts before done.

I found to praise the "Gift-Giver"
gave meaning and purpose to life,
so I praised Him in all of my writings
and He led me through sorrow and strife.
Now I use the "gift" that God gave me
to lead others gently along
and allow them to see His brightness,
and praise Him in words and in song.
What more can I do but to give Him
the best that I can in return
for the love that He's given so freely,
for in my heart it will always burn.
So until my eyes close forever,
my pencil will not cease to write
and create new ways to praise Him,
and do it with all of my might.

SEEDS OF LIFE

I planted a little seed today.
I had planted the seed before.
I watered it then with bits of wisdom
so that it could grow the more.

I watched it sprout in thirsty soil
then wither in time and die.
It made me sad to see shallow roots
and I could not help but cry.

Perhaps the seed I planted today
will take root in fertile soil.
I'll coax it with God's sunny love
and I'll not mind the toil.

I'll cultivate the weeds away
so there'll be more room to grow.
It'll take some time and effort too
but the fruits of labor will show.

No effort is wasted in words of love,
no time is given in vain.
The seeds of love from Jehovah's heart
are watered with His own rain.

I'll continue to plant the seeds of life
for it's the best that I can give.
The gift is not my own, but God's...
to help others eternally live.

+ + +

"Some fell upon stony places, where they had
not much earth..."
"And when the sun was up, they were scorched;
and because they had no root, they withered away."
Matthew 13:5a, 6 KJV

ROSES OF THE HEART

What can I say to tell you
the words that are in my heart,
or the joy I feel at seeing you
when we have been apart?

And how can I say with feeling
after years of wedded bliss,
the words that say "I love you"
and that it can't get better than this?

For though life has dealt some problems
and some years may have been lean,
you're still the one I long for,
the most beautiful person I've seen.

I know I don't often tell you
of the love that's in my heart,
so perhaps these simple words
is a place where I can start.

I LOVE YOU!

+ + +

For my husband, Charles.

TEACH ME TODAY

Teach me to do Your will, oh, God.
Show me the way to go.
Help me to find the road to Life.
Teach me what I should know.

Light the path of righteousness
that I may stumble no more.
Help me find the way to live.
Show me the life-giving door.

I am a speck of lowly sand
on the shore of teaming sin.
Wash my heart with Your pure love
and cleanse me from within.

Fill me with Your power of love,
then teach me to give it away.
Teach me forgiveness, cleanse my heart,
so that I may *live today!*

+ + +

"Wisdom is the prime thing. Acquire wisdom;
and with all that you acquire, acquire understanding."
Proverbs 4:7 NWT

QUESTIONS - ANSWERS

Did you know that God's Name is "Jehovah?"
Did you know that He loves every one
so much that, you know, He sent here below,
the life of His precious dear Son.

Did you know that God's Son's Name is "Jesus?"
Did you know that He loves us so much
that He ransomed His life with cruelty and strife
so His blood could keep us in touch?

Did you know we can have life eternal
on an earth that will become Paradise?
God will walk here each day if we live life His Way
and wipe every tear from our eyes.

What will you give to Jehovah God
in exchange for the "Gift" of His Son?
He looks from above for the return of your love
and will reward you when this life is done.

Sing praises to the One God, Jehovah.
Preach the gospel to hearts in despair.
Give hope to the lost who in turmoil are tossed.
Let them know that His love's always there.

Did you know that Jehovah won't leave us
to live in this world all alone?
He sent Jesus to share His love in pure prayer
and lead the way to a Paradise home.

+ + +

"For God loved the world so much that He gave
His only begotten Son, in order that everyone
exercising faith in Him might not be destroyed,
but have everlasting life.
John 3:16 NWT

RESURRECTION EXPECTATIONS

In the coming resurrection
when the world is clean and bright,
and we can see Jesus' glory
shine as if there was no night,
we will see our own dear loved ones
in their new perfected state.
All the world will feel God's love
and there'll be no room for hate.
Mom will meet her own sweet mother
who left her when she was so young.
Words of love for her long-missed mother
will flow freely from her tongue.
And as for me, I'll welcome daddy
and I'll teach him how to read
from the Bible that I cherish
and God's Word he'll learn to heed.
I'll introduce my own dear children
to the grandpa they never knew.
Oh, there'll be so much to tell him
and so many new things to do.
He'll be surprised at all the knowledge
of the Truth that I have learned
and that I became a Witness
of Jehovah that once he spurned.
But our Great God holds no grudges
for the things misunderstood.

He forgives and loves us dearly
for He knows our hearts are good.
We'll be able to show each other
all the Christian love God gives
as one by one we're resurrected
and in God's righteous world we'll live.
God will teach us to be tolerant
to the ones who went before.
We will show them all the wonders
of technology and so much more.
They will learn of our dear Savior
and the sacrifice He made.
They will shed hot tears of sorrow
to learn that for their sins He paid.
Oh, what joyful expectations
in Jesus Christ's millennial reign.
There'll be nothing left to sorrow
and only eternity to gain
for all those who will be faithful
in Christ's Kingdom from above.
Then He'll return it to Jehovah,
His Father and Author of all Love.

MAN'S DESTINY

How sad it makes Jehovah
when His children disobey.
Just like an earthly father,
it gives Him great dismay.

His children tend to grieve Him
in their wanton lust and sin,
giving Satan the invitation
to step up and walk right in.

If we deny His Sovereignty
and let Satan rule our nation,
we'll give him our permission
to rule to our ruination.

But if for right steadfast we stand,
Someday we'll realize
that we'll reside with Jehovah God
in an earthly Paradise.

MY COMFORT, MY JOY!

He put a song on my lips.
He put a melody in my soul.
He put His joy in my heart.
Such riches are yet untold.

He made the sun in dreary weather
to warm the innards of my being.
He brought us all in love together,
and sent the evil spirits fleeing.

Oh, such comfort my soul does feel
when Satan would steal my joy away.
I know the love of Jehovah is real.
He speaks to my heart whenever I pray.

+ + +

"for *this* day *is* holy unto our Lord: neither be
ye sorry; for the joy of the LORD Jehovah
is your strength."
Nehemiah 8:10b KJV

BIBLE QUOTATIONS are from the King James Version and the New World Translation of the Holy Scriptures listed below.

KJV... Genesis 1:1, 2...Job 26:7...Psalm 24:1...John14:21b...1Timothy1:16... Psalm 91:11...John 16:23...Psalm 46:10...Matthew 6:5...Jeremiah 31:12b... Job 9:16...Proverbs 17:17...Job 11:18...Isaiah 27:1...Romans10:13... Matthew13:5, 6...Matthew 7:1, 2...Isaiah 45:22, 23...Luke 9:26... Luke 11:9, 10...Hebrews 13:1, 2...Genesis 9:13a...Matthew 22:37, 38... II Corinthians 5:17...Proverbs17:22...Psalm118:1a...Matthew 28:20b... John3:16...John10:10b...Proverbs 18:15...Proverbs 15:13...Genesis 1:16... Matthew 21:22...Ecclesiastes 3:1...John 12:45...Jeremiah 29:13,14a... Matthew 21:22...John 14:6...Exodus 20:12..Joshua 1:5b...Job 8:13b, 14... Deuteronomy 6:6, 7...Matthew 14:23b...1 Corinthians 13:12...Psalm 62:7... Hebrews 13:5...Matthew 13:5a, 6...Nehemiah 8:10b.

NWT... James 2:23...James5:16...Ezekiel34:27a...Matthew6:1921... John16:33b...Jeremiah29:13...Psalm139:14,15a,16a,b... Ecclesiastes3:13...Psalm27:79...Proverbs22:6...Proverbs 4:7...John 3:16.

Biography of Evelyn B. Ryan

Evelyn Bonnie (Bankston) Ryan was born in Guntersville, Alabama on January 28, 1940 in a two room log cabin on top of "Little Mountain", so named by the Cherokee Indians before the turn of the century. A man by the name of "Taylor" bought the land and it became known as "Taylor's Mountain". Only five families lived on the mountain at that time.

When Evelyn was three her family moved to Baltimore, Maryland where she and her two sisters, Iva Gene and Barbara Ann, were raised. At seventeen years of age, Evelyn married a young service man named Charles Patrick Ryan and she traveled with him whenever she could. Three children were born to Charles and Evelyn during the twenty four years Charles was in the military. The oldest is Charles Patrick, Jr., then Patrick Alen, and last a daughter named Evelyn Marie. Charles served three tours in Germany and one in Viet Nam. His last tour in Germany resulted in a near-death accident that ended his army career. Once he and Evelyn's family returned to the United States, they bought a home in Bel Air, Maryland in 1974. They resided there for 37 years and then moved to Joppa, Maryland.

Evelyn's spiritual life is very important to her. She attended the Emmanuel Episcopal Church in Bel Air. She served as Emmanuel Ladies Chairperson for two years, taught Sunday school and also Vacation Bible School. She later attended many other denominational churches and finally settled in the Bel Air/Fallston Kingdom Hall of Jehovah's Witnesses in 1992 where she was baptized.

Evelyn has had a love of writing since she was a young girl. She wrote for a class newspaper called "The Junior Journal" and got her first taste of being an author. She loved writing stories from her imagination and spent many hours spinning tales at night, telling them to her two sisters. Later she learned to love rhyming words and began composing poems, most of them spiritual in nature. To date she has written more than five hundred poems. She sold one of her works entitled "The Farmer" to the Farm Woman News magazine in 1985. She also has five poems published in hard back books.

Evelyn worked as private secretary to Hershel Pell, editor of the D.O.E. Talent Times, with whom she co-authored a book entitled "Chronicles of the Pell Family." Evelyn has been writing for 55 years. It has always been her dream to become an accomplished writer of children's stories and books of poetry.

+ + + + + +